WAKE THE
F#CK UP

BRETT MORAN

WAKE THE F#CK UP

TRANSFORM YOUR LIFE INTO ONE EPIC ADVENTURE

WATKINS

Sharing Wisdom Since
1893

DEDICATION

This book is dedicated to Ella Louise! The little angel who woke me up when I needed it most. Thank you for helping Daddy with his transformation, you really saved my life and you're the kindest, funniest and cheekiest little monkey I know. You continue to teach me that life is one epic adventure and I love our time together because you remind me what's really important in life, such as unconditional love, kindness and connection. You can be anything you want to be, baby – always follow your heart.

This edition published in the UK and USA 2016 by
Watkins, an imprint of Watkins Media Limited
19 Cecil Court, London WC2N 4EZ

enquiries@watkinspublishing.co.uk

Design and typography copyright © Watkins Media Limited 2016
Text copyright © Brett Moran 2016

1 3 5 7 9 10 8 6 4 2

Typeset by Manisha Patel

Printed and bound in Finland

A CIP record for this book is available from the British Library

ISBN: 978-1-78028-896-3

www.watkinspublishing.com

CONTENTS

WHEN THE WAKE-UP CALL STARTS RINGING

'BELIEVE NOTHING. NO MATTER WHERE YOU READ IT, OR WHO SAID IT, EVEN IF I HAVE SAID IT, UNLESS IT AGREES WITH YOUR OWN REASON AND YOUR OWN COMMON SENSE.' The Buddha

5 JANUARY 1999

Parked up in my Fiat Bravo at 3am, I found myself breaking off white rocks for another crack pipe . . . I was high, paranoid and losing the plot. I hadn't slept in days and my mistrustful thoughts obsessed about the people, police and enemies out to get me. Each hit sent me further into a dark and cruel world and each delusional thought sent shudders of panic down my spine – the drugs had me hostage. I had a love-hate relationship with crack: the addictive side of me loved the artificial buzz and instant high; the real me hated what it was doing to my life – the suicidal lows, the deceitfulness, the withdrawal symptoms.

But in the next crazy, cracked-out moment, I suddenly got very clear . . . a voice started talking in my head that sounded nothing like the usual critical and destructive chatter that drove me mad. This new voice was louder but strangely softer, and it pierced through the negativity and the cunning and deceitful stories living inside my head. Up to that point, dealing drugs, getting high, scamming people and not giving a f#ck about anyone but me just felt normal, something I did, and who I was. The truth is I was lost in the chaotic world I had created but I didn't know how bad it was about to get – crack cocaine had sucked me in after my first pipe!

On this particular night, sitting there in my motor, I blew out a cloud of crack fumes and, as my brain buzzed on the last evil and delicious hit, I looked at my mate and told him what this new voice had said: 'I'm going to sort myself out and write a book.' He looked at me seriously for a moment then laughed and called me a 'nutter'! Quite right – too I was f#cked!

I get it. Nobody likes to be told to 'Wake the f#ck up!' But the title caught your attention, right? It's like saying to someone you might have got it wrong. Our ego screams, 'How f#cking dare you! Who do you think you are!' We defend our identity and behaviours until we're blue in the face. But waking up simply means gaining more knowledge, opening your mind and finding a better way of doing things so you can make you life easier. Because living a life you didn't consciously create or choose always gives you more of the same – whether it's being stuck in a job that sucks the life out of you, locked away in a prison cell, spending your whole life in debt, feeling trapped by drugs or any other addictive habits that 'seem' normal, being at a crossroads in your life, or simply following the crowd and going round in stressful circles. In a nutshell, waking up simply means setting yourself free.

Waking up is also a science and a process, and comes in many different shapes, sizes and stages. Having spent way too many years hitting way too many rock bottoms and starting over again, I know that anyone can wake up from any sleepy daydream or living nightmare they feel stuck in and create something far more epic for themselves. Anyone can change any behaviour, take control of their life and live for the better, if they choose to put in the work, of course! I believe there is the power and potential inside everyone on Earth to start again and create a life that ignites a fire in their belly, and, when they do, wonderful things begin to shift inside and life changes naturally – and it's never too late to wake up!

After ten years of personal transformation, I've discovered that waking the f#ck up is about getting back in the driving seat of your life. It takes you out of this cloudy fog and gives you more choices and freedom. It puts you back in touch with who you really are at a very deep level so you can choose who you want to become, what you want to achieve and how you want to show up in the world. Deep down we all want to be free from the pressure of the never-ending treadmill. We want to feel more from life than the flat line that has hypnotized millions of people. I also believe that it's our inner strength, the love in our hearts and the power of our imaginations that set us free. It might not seem like it now, or feel like too big a leap from where you are to where you want to be, but there is something inside you that can guide your life and help you activate your full potential.

So what do you want to do? Change? To step it up, learn new skills and make life more meaningful, or ignore that inner calling and carry on plodding down the same old path?

Choose not to change and it's obvious what happens. We get the same results year after year. Same amount of money, same addictions, same heavy feelings, same unwanted thoughts and the same relationships. We give up on our dreams and stay trapped in society's hypnotic illusions of happiness and running faster than ever before in this rat race just to keep up with the 'social norms' but getting nowhere.

I know how it feels to get to that point, knowing that something needs to change, but feeling intimidated and scared by it. You may feel like you've lost your way. Not sure which way to turn. Doubt yourself and your ability to succeed. Like your spark has gone or life is all about paying the bills and doing what everyone else is doing – while all the time feeling like something's missing and there must be more to it than waking up each day and going through the motions. If life seems to be slipping away from you right now, you feel flat and lost or you're ready for the next step and you really want more, then it's definitely time to wake the f#ck up.

In my experience, feeling lost, flat, at rock bottom, frustrated, pissed off, stuck, or simply bored means it's time to look within, pay attention to your inner itch, and connect to your inner voice because when you do then something epic is just around the corner! If you have this book in your hands then you have it for a bigger reason than you think. You are on the edge of transformation, and something is calling you to step it up, now is your time!

Let the real adventure begin!

BIG LOVE,
Brett xxx

WAKE THE F#CK UP

'THE BEST WAY TO MAKE YOUR DREAMS COME TRUE IS TO WAKE UP.' Paul Valéry

13 NOVEMBER 2001

I was 19 when my 17-year-old girlfriend fell pregnant with Ella in Tenerife. Originally I'd fled there because I was due to appear in court for my second drink-driving offence. I'd also been joyriding a stolen car at the time so I knew I'd get sent down. My mates had done time in prison and it wasn't for me. I had a criminal record for possession of class-A drugs, racism, affray, the usual story for a kid growing up in my south London neighbourhood, but I wasn't ready for prison, so when Dad offered to help me do a runner to Tenerife and pay for my plane ticket, I jumped at the chance and packed my bags. On the day I was due to fly out, my solicitor phoned to tell Dad that the police had screwed up the evidence and I'd been let off on a technicality. They threw the case out of court and I flew to Tenerife a free man, sold timeshares on the beach, got drunk in the sun and took ecstasy.

By the time Mum and my girlfriend flew out to visit me, I was ready to come home. I felt homesick and missed my mates, so when it was time for my Mum and girlfriend to leave I flew back with them. As soon as I got back I was up to no good! Mum and Dad had split up, Dad was on the coke and Mum had moved out so I was a loose cannon. In the end my childhood home became a drug den as Dad and I got bang on it! After being home for a few weeks and watching Dad lose the plot on coke, I started planning how I could head off to Ibiza . . . Little did I know that nine months later I'd be getting the biggest wake-up call of my life!

Exhausted from giving birth, my girlfriend was fast asleep. Suddenly it was just Ella and me connecting in the silence. I held her in my arms and, as I looked down at her tiny little features, my heart melted. Her eyes were filled with so much life, joy and wisdom, like tiny universes sparkling with pure magic and light, and in that moment I felt so clear and connected that the world outside seemed to disappear. It was just Ella and me! Her nose, ears and fingers were so cute and tiny. I couldn't get my head around how small she was. She was beautiful and perfect in so many ways. I was speechless and the unconditional love I felt for this little miracle of life blew me away. A strange and wonderful sensation swam through my body and I felt this inner emotion I had never felt before. As the tears rolled down my cheeks, something unlocked inside me and my heart opened up.

As my heart ignited, Ella's unconditional love swallowed me up. Nothing in the world mattered any more. In that moment I knew I'd found the ultimate buzz. It was pure, authentic and real, and I never wanted it to end . . . I was so thankful and grateful for life. A huge feeling of appreciation welled up in the back of my throat and behind my eyes. Tears gently rolled off my chin and landed on Ella's tiny babygrow. Unexpectedly, out of nowhere, reality kicked in and this negative thought flashed into my mind: 'How the f#ck can I look after this beautiful little girl when I can't even look after myself?' I was a drug dealer, criminal and waste of space!'

I haven't always seen life as one epic miracle . . . I grew up in a rough housing estate in Carshalton on the outskirts of south London. Living for the weekends, committing crime and dealing drugs were just normal to us kids – and we grew up fast. The local pubs could turn nasty in a matter of minutes, if you got on the wrong side of someone. Locals got drunk. Stabbed people over nothing. And your street credit was far more valuable then your life!

Getting up to no good and following the crowd was part of the territory. A gang of us would roam the streets. Do graffiti. Smash up bus shelters. Get into fights. Nick car stereos. Drink booze. Smoke. And take stuff that wasn't ours! As we got older we robbed shops, nicked the cars, sold the drugs and went on to harder drugs, armed robberies and more violence. Carshalton was the cards I got dealt. For a young kid growing up it was fun, exciting and an adventure, it was my first buzz. It was all I knew back then! But after the experimenting with drugs wore off, addiction kicked in and the fun disappeared. In the end I felt alone, empty and worthless!

The idea of looking after a baby with all the responsibilities involved didn't stop me dealing drugs, getting drunk and fighting at the weekends. In fact, after Ella was born I got worse. The crime and drugs got harder. It was going to be a few years and many crazy adventures before I really stepped it up to became a decent father to Ella. But the night she was born something changed deep inside me. Ella reignited something in my heart and woke me up!

So what does an ex-crack head know about waking up and transforming himself? Fast-forward a decade and I'm free, buzzing off life and higher than ever before – naturally, by the way! I've been clean and sober for seven years, I don't eat meat or watch TV, and I've chosen to remain celibate for the last three years! I know what you're thinking, 'What a boring f#ck!' To be honest, I've never felt so high, happy, energetic, loved-up, connected, pure and healthy. Every day I wake up with a real genuine buzz inside me because I feel free, tuned into the magic and love, and the miracle of life and spend most of my days wanting to explode with excitement. Truthfully, I feel so blessed I'm alive and sharing this epic adventure with you, and it keeps getting better, I keep going higher, and there are no comedowns!

To cut a long story short, I went from a crack head to clean, drug dealer to life coach, prison inmate to public speaker, binge drinker to yoga addict, car thief to author and documentary maker. I'll be sharing a number of my stories in this book, too. In the last 10 years of working as a life coach, giving talks, running workshops and now selling online programmes to people all around the world, I've helped countless people wake the f#ck up and create better lives: from homeless heroin addicts smoking smack on the streets to diamond dealers struggling to find happiness; troubled teens to the 30–60 crowd looking for more passion and purpose; DJs and artists looking for more creativity and parents struggling to connect and bond with their children. I've been paid to go back in to prisons and give talks to inmates (thankfully they let me back out!). I've featured in a number of personal development books on healing and transformation, raised thousands of pounds for charitable causes and volunteered with vulnerable and disadvantaged people. And I recently starred in a film with Richard Branson and Jack Canfield talking about change and waking up!

So if you're looking for some tools to help you improve the quality of your life, some guidance on taking control of your mind and how to ignite more energy and happiness then you're in the right place! I'm not looking for a trophy or a pat on the back; I help people because I'm addicted to this new path and love seeing others break free from the crowd. I also know the importance of waking up and giving back to others what you've learnt. It teaches us so much about life and makes us feel alive! To be honest, every client or person I've helped along the way has helped me become the person I am today. I am deeply grateful for everyone I have ever connected to! For me, waking up has always been a two-way process and I'm still learning just as much as anyone else.

What I've learnt from a decade of personal transformation and studying this path like a nutty professor is in this book – the blueprint for waking up and creating one epic life. Some of my methods might seem a bit weird and wacky, but nearly everything worth having in life is found outside the box . . . You may find, however, that waking up also means you start going against the crowd in your own way because when we do that – when we try new things – we learn more about who we are and how life really works. We wake up and move way beyond the limitations holding us back in life. If you're ready for change then you'll learn the exact strategies that will help you charge forwards and smash it, including the ones I still use every day!

My plan is simple: I'll show you how to rocket-fuel your life to the next level – whether that's a major life transformation or simply escaping negativity and creating more peace, happiness and freedom. That's exactly what *Wake the F#ck Up* is all about.

IT'S ABOUT DOING YOUR OWN THING . . .

Waking up is a personal journey for each of us. No two paths are the same, but the process of awakening is exactly the same for everyone. The first thing you'll usually need to face is quite often the thing you've been avoiding the most. You! It may be something small, like paying more attention to the negative thoughts in your head, or re-evaluating the people you hang out with and how you spend your free time, or something more major, like ditching the job that's tormenting you, leaving a loveless relationship or taking a leap of faith, finding your purpose and following your dreams. And if you're not sure why you're feeling stuck in life, or which way to go, then paying close attention to those little nudges you feel, the little voice whispering in your ear, or the gut feeling trying to steer you in a new direction, is the start of your wake-up call.

I heard that voice when I was smoking crack but I laughed it off. I felt those gut instincts to change when Ella was born, but I ignored them and followed the crowd. These warning signs are always appearing before us, trying to help us wake up, make better choices, and create an easier and more fulfilling life. We just need to pay attention and tune into them. As you start to look within and take new actions towards your chosen path, you'll find that one small change can lead to gigantic breakthroughs and that all of the challenges and obstacles are tests to help you grow and succeed. Suddenly, life becomes a game and starts to feel really epic again! You have more energy and passion, you feel free and light and the adventure becomes almost effortless. The dramas and negative patterns seem to fade out of your life and your days become more enjoyable and productive.

Some people fear this change so much that they never escape the rat race and repeat the same negative patterns year after year, even though they hate them. Instead of asking, 'What if there is another way to live my life?', they defend their negative behaviours and stay slaves to their critical thoughts. They spend their whole lives fighting themselves, convincing themselves they are right or moaning about the system, battling with cruel and unwanted thoughts, or making the politicians, immigrants or the weather take the blame for their unhappiness. In the end, they're the only ones losing out, and often become jealous and bitter towards those who achieve more with their time here, and hating others and talking behind their backs.

A WORD OF WARNING

When you finally decide enough is enough and make the decision to get more from life and follow your heart then the people around you will change too. Everybody secretly dreams of achieving more and most of us want to better ourselves and live more fully, but many never take the leap or make the move. Perhaps they don't believe they can do it or simply feel lost and confused, ruled by their negative self-talk and society's rules, so they never change and belittle those who do. As you take control of your life and choose to get more from it, you may also experience others judging you negatively for it, but don't let this stop you; just smile and keep on moving. This is your life and it means you are on the right track and breaking the mould!

THE AWAKENING

While millions of people are trapped in their own pain and suffering, going round in circles, chasing their tails, millions more are waking up and discovering there is a more epic way of living their lives. That they can follow their dreams, make the world a better place and break away from society's stresses. Just the other month, I was at Box Park in Shoreditch getting some vegan grub when I overheard a group of young lads talking about the shift in consciousness and how to make the world a better place. They were chatting about how we need to think more about animal cruelty, how to love one another unconditionally and how this can create peace on the planet. It blew me away! When I was that age, I was up to no good smoking crack! Nowadays we have teenagers breaking the mould and making the world a better place by their choices and actions. It's even become cool to go against the crowd and not follow the herd. But it's not just vegan gangsters who want to leave this planet in a better state than they found it. From city bankers who have given up the chase, pensioners volunteering in soup kitchens, inmates in prison cells, single mums and everyday people like you and me, we're starting to question the myths of the old world and how things 'should' be done, and instead choosing something more meaningful for their lives and the world we all share!

More and more people are waking up from the illusion of the human 'race'.

When you finally stop to think about it and ask bigger questions such as, 'How's my life working out for me?', 'Am I really happy with the path I'm on?', 'Do I want to create something new, fun and exciting today?', you start to investigate more deeply what needs to change in your life and in the world. You see what patterns you need to break, find discomfort in your comfort or feel this yearning for more. And then your adventure really begins! Anyone can go through the motions, plod along and turn a blind eye to the madness, but is that really going to create more bliss in our lives?

It's safe to say in the last 20 years we have had a huge shift in consciousness. We didn't have all this information at our fingertips. But thanks to forward thinkers and the digital revolution, our world has radically transformed. Because of this it's easier to access new information, connect to others who are waking up and spread a positive message.

This shift in consciousness is on the rise too, so think of this as your opportunity to join the inner revolution and really discover something new within you. Once you make the decision to investigate a little deeper, become willing to open your mind and finally go after the life you secretly dream about, then the rest will happen naturally. We were born to evolve and grow like nature and as soon as we align with who we are destined to become, life becomes easy. When you wake up, you transform into the person screaming to get out of you and the negative voice screaming at you begins to fade away!

LOOKING WITHIN

I think one of the main reasons why so many people stay stuck is because they never look within or take the time to get to know themselves at a deeper level. Instead they live what I call 'external lives'. In other words, they're so distracted by all the information outside of themselves and the need to keep up with everyone else, addicted to the gossip, controlled by the ego, or glued to the TV, keeping up with fashion, indulging in harmful habits and being more concerned about the external world and how they look, that they forget who they are at a deeper level and the powerful voice inside them becomes faint. They block it out.

I'm certainly not judging anyone, because it's all too easy to get caught on the treadmill of work and life, to get stuck in the laziness of society and zone out. The problem is, when we believe that happiness, love and peace are something external, we can chase instant gratification rather than creating long-term bliss. This is why many people end up doing jobs they don't like just to buy things they don't need or want, and lose touch with who they really are and the things that make them feel happy and alive!

What's more, we are subconsciously brainwashed by marketers and big brands to keep running with everyone else – to have the latest car, the best house on the street, the next gadget. It's so exhausting and stressful that we spend the rest of the time trying to escape from life and wishing we could be free. By which I mean, we might slump with a beer or a bottle of wine to unwind, or roll a joint and zone out in front of the TV in an attempt to relax or book a week's holiday in the sun just to get away! Except we don't relax or get away . . . we watch TV and fill our minds with even more negative news stories, come home after the week in the sun and feel fed up, get addicted to more gossip and watch how the celebrities are living their lives – we come back to the same old patterns we left but we have a nicer tan! Thanks to certain media outlets, we start to believe that the world is a scary and dangerous place; life feels harsh and tough and we let our hair down and numb out by watching *Eastenders* on a TV screen the size of a small cinema or getting smashed on the weekends. But is any of it actually making us any happier, is it really adding any value to our lives?

As you will read in this book, I'm not saying you shouldn't have stuff or you should cut yourself off from the world and lock yourself away in a cave. Life is a celebration, have material goals and enjoy them, but if you really want to feel alive and touch the magic of life then start looking within. The external stuff will always come and go but your inner universe will be with you for the rest of your life. I couldn't think of anything worse than to have all the stuff you wanted but not understand the stuff inside you. Looking inside ourselves and reconnecting to who we are at a core level is how we find the answers. One day we have to wake up and listen to our inner guide and ask, what do I really want from my life?

HOW TO USE THIS BOOK

Reading a book won't change your life, but it can challenge, trigger, inspire and motivate you, and then it's about putting in the work and taking action when the time comes. My advice is to be open and unlearn everything you've been taught. Take one step at a time and question everything, especially your negative and limiting thoughts!

Studies show that keeping a journal and writing our thoughts and insights down can help us to learn more and absorb information. Personally I've had a number of journals and they have been the key to my personal success. When I flick back through them a few years later, I'm blown away by how much they've impacted my life. I'm always writing down my thoughts, feelings and dreams! So I want you to grab a new journal too, take notes and follow along with the exercises. Don't skip any of them, no matter how weird or wacky they sound; write down what comes up, how you are feeling, do the work and ponder over your answers, because this will ignite long-lasting change and transform your destiny!

I'm not saying it's going to be easy or happen overnight, I'm not even saying you should believe me – after all, I was a crackhead! Challenge me, at least give the exercises a good go, then make your mind up. But I can guarantee you this: looking within and waking the f#ck up will be the best decision you ever make. In years to come you will look back and thank yourself for stepping out of the box and taking control of your life. Every time I see one of my clients step it up and charge towards their dreams, it blows me away to see how much they achieve. Before we begin this new journey together, to whet your appetite, here are eight of the beneficial actions you'll start to practise as you work your way through this book:

#1 TAKE CONTROL OF YOUR MIND!

The monkey mind can be a little f#cker if it is not controlled! But when you learn simple yet profound ways of thinking and living inside your head, it can become a state of peace and harmony. You can separate yourself from any negative thoughts and stories and start to build a positive relationship with your inner voice and talk to yourself in a more constructive way!

#2 TUNE INTO THE PRESENT MOMENT!

Nowness is where the bliss is found because you can't feel happy or at peace when you're worrying about the past or stressing about the future. The more you engineer your consciousness and tune into the nowness of life, the louder your inner voice becomes and it guides you towards better outcomes in your life.

#3 GET CRYSTAL CLEAR!

Taking control of your life and creating a new vision for your future will give you more direction and purpose in the now. Your day-to-day life becomes more positive because you'll have something bigger to live for and you'll become more productive as you dream higher and act bolder. Instead of feeling lost, bored or unsure, you feel focused, bang on target and determined!

#4 EXPEL YOUR FEARS!

We all secretly dream of a better life, whether that involves more money, more energy, more time off, more happiness, fun and adventure, ot better health. The biggest illusion holding us back is fear. It will kid you into not taking action time and time again! As you read this book and do the exercises, you'll learn how to eliminate any deep-rooted fears that are blocking you from your personal success so you can leap forwards into your new vision!

#5 BREAK YOUR NEGATIVE PATTERNS!

I don't know about you, but repeating unwanted patterns drives me insane! But as you become aware of your deeper needs and become more conscious of your actions you'll feel empowered to replace a lifetime of negative habits with healthy and productive behaviours that move you closer to your goals.

#6 IGNITE INSANE ENERGY!

When you strategically engineer your energy you'll feel lighter and faster! Your energy will shoot through the roof. You'll feel pure inside and spring into action. You'll also notice you can get more done in half the time and have more stamina and oomph to make sh#t happen and charge towards your vision!

#7 TUNE INTO MORE BLISS!

Taking control of your path in life and waking up has more benefits then I could ever write about! I guess the biggest shift I've noticed in my short time here is how joyful and happy we can really become! By making bliss a habit, you start to experience life more deeply and feel joy for no other reason then being alive! The simple things excite you,

you notice so much more in life and the daily miracles that ignite your buzz become your drug!

#8 FEEL IMMENSE LOVE!

When you wake up you realize love is the answer! It's all we crave, want and desire. Everything else is an illusion! This book will show you the three stages of self-love and if you are ready for it, it will offer you a concept that tunes you into a deeper level of oneness. Love in its highest form! You start treating yourself and others with more care, affection and respect and you become magnetic and attract what or who you really desire, and life really does become one epic miracle!

....

Throughout this book you'll find lots of quick-hit exercises. They are marked with a target icon ⊕, because they really help to focus your efforts to wake the f#ck up. Many of these exercises involve the use of a journal, so if you don't have one already, get one now!

There are also various 'WTF' sections, marked with a hashtag #, which introduce you to some of the influential thinkers and philosophies that have made a difference to me, and I believe can have a positive effect on you as well.

CHAPTER 1

ENGINEERING YOUR MIND

'WE BECOME WHAT WE THINK ABOUT.' Earl Nightingale

23 MAY 2003

'Guilty!'

'*WTF?*' Standing in the dock, I felt weak and sick to my stomach when I heard the prick stick me on remand. *'I'm not prison material. I'm hardly one of the f#cking Kray Twins or a Great Train Robber,'* I thought as the security men grabbed both my arms to take me away. Arrested for my third driving offence, I was about to be sent down for the first time. I was shocked and terrified!

Mixed feelings rioted through my body. Ella was only two years old and I knew I'd let her down big time. I was still selling and taking drugs. Nothing had changed! Mum was sitting opposite me in court crying her eyes out. She couldn't even look at me. I felt mortified, but it was too late for that! Standing in the dock, knowing I was heading to prison, I couldn't show any signs of weakness. *'F#ck that, I'll get killed,'* I thought, so I stood straight up, manned up and walked down to the cells. Inside I was sh#tting myself!

Up to that point, like so many people, I'd played the cards I was dealt. My environment shaped me and I wasn't aware that life could be any other way. Never thinking there could be a better way or there was more than Carshalton. I'm not complaining, or blaming anyone whatsoever. I made the choices that led to that black day in court, I did the crime, but I didn't have a clue how to do things differently, so I plodded through life, controlled by my negative beliefs and unwanted patterns.

I never asked 'Why am I here? What's my purpose in life? Who am I?' I'd never thought about my responsibilities as a father or what I was teaching Ella. I blocked it out by taking drugs. I kept drugs in the house and did dodgy deals, as I chased one of the biggest illusions – living for an artificial buzz. No one ever told me there was another way to feel good about being me. That I could take control of my life, separate from my thoughts or change my habits.

Sitting in the sweatbox, heading towards prison, my thoughts raced out of control. My mind flew all over the place: would I get jumped, raped, stabbed or bullied? I suppressed my emotions but felt distraught. I could hear the other soon-to-be inmates kicking off, shouting and swearing at the security men, punching their cages, but I didn't say a word and just sat staring out of the window, watching the world flash past, thinking, 'How on Earth did it get to this?'

Nothing can prepare you for stepping into a prison cell. The grey, lifeless walls, the cold concrete floor and a tiny window with thick bars become your depressing reality. As the screw locked the door behind me, a chill went down my spine. My freedom was gone, the air felt suffocating and my head and emotions were spinning. Little did I know that I was about to discover two things I never expected to find in prison – heroin and spirituality!

I'd always thought of heroin as a dirty drug. As a kid I remembered seeing the local smack heads walking up and down Thornton Road looking like lost souls and it put me off the nasty drug. As I got older, some of the older lads I used to hang out with turned to heroin and were sucked in from the get go. But when the fat prick in the cell next door latched on to me and offered me some brown and gave me the tools to chase the dragon, I didn't think twice about accepting. I was desperate for something, anything, to switch off the crazy thoughts inside my head, even if it went against my better judgement. I just wanted to escape!

Heroin wasn't for me. It cleared my mind a bit, gave me a better night's sleep, but when I woke up my problems were still there and I felt achy and worse than before. So I smoked it for a few weeks then told the dealer to jog on before it turned into a habit. I approached a screw and asked to be moved off the 'drug' wing because I knew temptation would always get the better of me. For once I was making a positive step towards change, but I was told to 'Deal with it!'

The next day I wrote a note to the screws and stuck it in the request box. The note said I feared for my life, that people on the wing were going to stab me because I owed them money. The story worked. They moved me the same day and that's when I found my next drug, spirituality!

THE MIND: WHAT WE THINK, WE BECOME.

We are thinking and feeling machines, which means we also have the ability to direct our thoughts to get better outcomes in our lives. The freedom to choose what you think can never be taken away from you, so engineering your mind is about learning to access that power at will. Each us of is creating his or her reality in their mind and so our thoughts are also the most powerful force in the universe because they can truly help us create and design a life we really want to experience. Anyone can expand their mind and direct the energy of their thoughts. When you take control of the power inside your head, you can rise above the negative thoughts and the limiting stories you tell yourself and create more peace, abundance and joy and put the epic back in your adventure.

Your thoughts may seem like they're invisible, you can't see them, but you know how much this energy whizzing around inside your head affects your life. Good or bad, happy or positive, light or dark, everything you're experiencing in your life right now is a reflection of the thoughts you think and have been thinking for many years. Your mind can create peace on Earth, but left to its own devices it can also create hell on Earth!

Everything starts out in our heads, so cultivating a more positive and calmer mind is the linchpin of this book. Waking up boils down to learning to switch your thoughts on and off when you need to, and uncovering any old loops that have been holding you back in life. In doing this, you'll also learn how to separate from the ego and create more awareness.

With a calm, healthy mind and strategic thinking patterns you can get your imagination to work for you rather than against you. The mind can become such a blissful place when you know how to engineer it and build a positive relationship with it. Rather than being a slave or victim to your thoughts, you start to steer your life in any direction you choose to think!

ADDICTED TO THINKING

Our thoughts travel 930,000 times faster than the sound of our voice. Within a split second you can be thinking about your first date, who he or she was and where you went, then the next second visualizing your life 10 years in the future or your next holiday. Thoughts are quicker than emails: think something and boom it's in your inbox (or out in the universe). In your mind's eye you can hop from London, to Africa, and then on to the US before you can spell Jamaica!

I'm sure your thoughts have driven you crazy once or twice too! You know those days when it feels like you can't switch off your mind and it seems out of control. You obsess about something or someone, or how wrongly you've been treated, or how right you are and end up having a full-blown conversation with yourself inside your head. Or maybe you worry about your future, your health, your children's education or the feelings you just can't shake off and snap out of because your mind refuses to switch off. This is what I call 'stinking thinking', but have you ever wondered where it comes from?

THE EGO VS. THE MIND

For most of us, our stinking thinking is usually down to our ego, or personality. Your ego is your thoughts, beliefs and attitudes and it develops when we're still babies. Its main purpose is to help us survive. A fast learner, the ego sucks up information from our parents, our environment and peers – this is called 'conditioning'. Most parents unconsciously 'condition' their children and teach them what to think. The trouble is that early conditioning affects how we show up in life and how we think. By the time we are adults, the ego is often no longer fit for purpose. Instead of being a helpful cheerleader guiding us through life, it is often our worst critic: a writhing mass of limiting thoughts and negative beliefs. As quite young children, and from some of the best parents in the world, we can become conditioned to believe all sorts of crap about ourselves and then spend our days tormenting and criticizing ourselves for being 'bad', 'lazy', 'useless', 'stupid', and so on. With all the unhelpful thoughts and limiting beliefs that have been conditioned into our heads, no wonder our thoughts seem so real and life seems so hard at times. I see the ego as an addict, addicted to thoughts, hungry for distraction and feeding off negativity. It never ends, it's always clucking!

Until the ego is tamed, it will rule your life and, chances are, hold you back from what you really want, but when you take away your inner addict's fuel, the negative thoughts, it loses its power over you.

When you learn to separate from your ego and engineer the true power in between your ears, the negative thoughts and limiting beliefs fade away, you expose your limited conditioning and your mind becomes a tool for change, freedom and success. The problem most people struggle with is that they believe the hype inside their minds and act according to their thoughts. Even if they didn't choose them! Think about it: When did you last challenge the thoughts in your head? Or choose new ones or cultivate awareness for what your mind was telling you?

The truth is, it's really easy to tune into this inner negative conversation and become addicted to old thinking patterns. These are like chewing gum for the ego, which feeds off stress, worries about the future, old negative fears and pains from the past, and gets its fix with critical, bitchy and judgemental thoughts. The more addicted you are to stinking thinking, albeit unknowingly, the stronger the ego becomes and the more it feeds its habit. I for one know if you were to hear some of my stray thoughts, I'd be locked up in a straitjacket! The trick, however, to recognizing what's real inside your head and what's not comes in developing some awareness about your thoughts.

⊕ **Challenge your thoughts**

The next time your thoughts flash into your head and feed your addictive ego with self-criticism, fear or negativity, stop them by challenging them. Talk back to them and break your old stinking-thinking cycle. Choose not to follow your thoughts. Then ask yourself the following:

* Are my thoughts true?

* Are they worth thinking right now?

If you answer 'no' to both questions then you know they're a load of nonsense and you should choose to let them go as quickly as they popped into your mind.

Our emotions are also a reflection of our thinking, while our actions and behaviours are consequences of our thinking, so if you're feeling crappy and struggling in any area of your life then it's time to check in with what your thoughts are saying to you and start questioning whether they're true.

If it's true that most people are addicted to their thoughts and listening to the same old tape loop they've been telling themselves year after year, over and over again, then it's no wonder that they never experience anything new in life, have a moment of peace or live to their full potential. Our thoughts can be pretty damaging and negative, so start to be vigilant about what you're thinking and don't let your thoughts beat you up, drill you down, make you feel unloved, or criticize and condemn you. When you bring this awareness to your thoughts, you can then start cultivating more positive ways of thinking so that your thoughts become potent and powerful, encouraging and motivating, successful and abundant. We can literally cheer ourselves on, think more clearly, become our best friends and direct our attention to greater places.

Your mind is the key to your personal success!

A WANDERING MIND

Something else to be aware of is the randomness of your thinking. Put the book down for a minute and stop reading. Set a timer on your phone for one minute. Then close your eyes and for the next 60 seconds watch your mind wander. Observe your thoughts without any judgement and become aware of how they wander. When you're done come back to the book.

How 'real' did your thoughts feel? And what if I told you that your thoughts and feelings are just a bunch of chemical reactions and impulses fired off and triggered by the information all around us, such as other people's actions, the environments you find yourself in, the news, media, and the gossip you expose yourself to. Your thoughts are also fired up by all the thoughts you have thought over the years. Which I'm sure are in the gazillions!

Did you know we have over 60,000 thoughts every day and 80 per cent of those are the same as yesterday? What's more, 80 per cent of those 60,000 thoughts are negative! When you think about it, just looking at a certain image on the TV or a computer screen can fill you with joy, lust, rage or disgust (or all of them, depending what you're looking at!). Or when we watch movies, the mind enters the role of the character, and our emotions are tugged when a character dies or falls in love. In fact, you don't even need to look at an image on a screen or watch a movie because you can imagine certain scenarios or old memories in your head right now and feel your mind and body react. Think about the birth of your baby, or imagine your little niece or nephew smiling at you and you'll feel happy, warm and loving. Whatever we focus our minds, we will always receive and feel different emotions.

When you closed your eyes and let your wandering mind take over, did you notice how random your thoughts were? How many thoughts did you think, where did they take you? Chances are you were thinking about what you did today, what's for dinner tonight, what's the point of this exercise, or what you've got to do tomorrow. Some people live in the past, others live in the future, some are thinking about themselves and how they are feeling, while others think about what others think of them and how other people are thinking and feeling. Left to its own devices, the mind will drift and wander all over the place so part of waking the f#ck up is learning how to shift your mind in a more helpful direction. So every now and then take a minute or two just to observe what your mind is doing and recognize your thoughts without any judgement. Just see where it goes, what you were thinking and stop thinking and breathe!

You don't have to follow your thoughts into the darkness! You always have a choice and the power to break through your thought patterns.

Of course, my mind still wanders like everyone else's out there. I've just learnt how to control it and not to react to it as much. I've spent years training and rewiring my mind to think more clearly, calmly and positively. I'll share some of the mantras I use to help me rise above the madness and negative thoughts in my mind later in this chapter. It might sound hard for some people to believe, but I haven't owned a TV for over 10 years. I never read the newspapers, and I'm very choosy who I hang out with and how I engage in certain conversations. Why? Because if it's all doom, gloom, judgement and gossip, and I don't want my mind infected with negativity. Our minds are like sponges and we soak up every piece of information around us, whether that's images in the paper, gossip from friends or fear and hate in the news. If we're not careful we'll become addicted to other people's views and opinions about who we are and the world we all live in.

TAMING THE MIND

If you find you have a voice in your head then you're normal; it's how you choose to control that voice, or your voices, and separate yourself from the pointless and negative ones that can make all the difference. Taming the monkey mind is the key to transformation; because otherwise, just like a monkey swinging from tree to tree, your thoughts will swing from one critical, obsessive, judgemental and disapproving thought to the next!

In Buddhism, there's a practice called 'mindfulness' and its purpose is to help us become aware of the monkey mind and observe our thoughts and the stories we tell ourselves without judgement. It's pretty easy to do too. You simply pay attention to the thoughts swirling around inside your head and choose not to follow them or identify with them. Breaking away from the non-stop thoughts in our head connects us to the magic of life – taking us into the moment, the now-ness of life. The now is where bliss and peace are found and we'll be delving more deeply into mindfulness in Chapter 2. What you'll find as you start to cultivate this more peaceful mindset is that you start to weed out the negative thoughts, you begin to understand your mind and recognize what triggers those old stinking-thinking patterns. You start to realize that you don't have to react to those thoughts, you can chill out and watch your thoughts float past like clouds in the sky.

....

⊙ Your thoughts are guests

Close your eyes and take a few deep breaths. Now I want you to imagine that your mind is a hotel and all the whirling thoughts and feelings in your mind are guests, each with its own personality and character, and like all guests they come and go. You may have guests who are on a stag or hen night and are acting crazy and wild, some of them might like to moan and groan about everything, some might be children who are full of beans and excited to be staying in such a magnificent hotel. Acknowledge each of your guests in turn and then, when you are ready, watch them leave. Just like your thoughts and feelings, all guests leave in the end. They come and go; come and go so choose not to get too attached to them.

When thoughts and feelings start swirling around your mind, close your eyes for a moment and remember you're the hotel, your thoughts and feelings are only guests!

Being more mindful of your thoughts and realizing they are not you is the key to separating from the ego and negative thinking. As your awareness of your mind grows, you'll start to uncover the story that you've been telling yourself about who you are and what you're capable of – and start to see through the illusion of the conditioning that created it. In turn, you'll find that you react less because you've awoken to the fact that you are more than just the sum of the thoughts and feelings and stories whizzing around inside your head.

◉ Using a mantra to interrupt negative thoughts

The next time random thoughts start to make your head busy, or make you feel foggy, guilty, bad, inadequate, insane, out of control or any other negative emotion, interrupt the thoughts by repeating one of these simple mantras.

* 'I am not my thoughts. I am not my thoughts. I am not my thoughts.'
* 'My thoughts are not real. My thoughts are not real. My thoughts are not real.'
* 'It's just a story. It's just a story. It's just a story.'

You can use mantras to interrupt all sorts of unhelpful behaviours and feelings too. For example, next time you catch yourself about to snap in anger, start judging or beating yourself up, or any other habitual cycles for that matter, just stop and start repeating a simple mantra to interrupt the pattern. For example, you might say:

* 'I am not my feelings. I am not my feelings. I am not my feelings.'
* 'I am not my behaviours. I am not my behaviours. I am not my behaviours.'
* 'I am not my actions. I am not my actions. I am not my actions.'

You might have to say these mantras over and over again to quiet your mind, but I guarantee over time they will work their magic and you'll spend more time being in the space in between your thoughts and feelings rather than identifying with them. I've been using these mantras since I left prison and when my mind gets too busy or my feelings get heavy or I slip back into a pattern, I repeat them over and over until I see through the story in my mind. I remind myself I am the space in between and my thoughts and feelings always come and go. Even the positive ones!

....

Meet Michael

Michael was highly medicated and had been given a dual diagnosis by the mental health team. Labelled a paranoid drug addict with schizophrenia and bipolar, to me he was just Michael and we got on well. At the time I was his key worker and he used to come into the drop-in centre once a week for acupuncture and meditation. I could tell his mind was always wandering and working overtime. He couldn't sit still, his eyes darted all over the place and he spoke at 100mph, shooting from one topic to the next. He used to tell me about the stories and thoughts inside his head and wasn't too sure which ones were real any more.

One particular day, the session started out as usual. I lit an incense stick, stuck the acupuncture needles in his ears, and started a Buddhist meditation. For the next 20 minutes we sat together and focused on our breathing. I guided him through the basics, suggested he watch his thoughts without judgement and let them float away like the clouds in the sky. Just 30 minutes later at the end of the session, I opened my eyes to a brand new Michael. He looked completely Zen and peaceful. He was glowing and said, 'Brett, that's the first time I've felt calm and not listened to my thoughts.'

I'm not a medical doctor but I do know that if Michael can find a moment of peace and learn how to control his mind, anyone can.

 # THE POWER OF ZEN

Mindfulness and meditation have been the subject of intense study in the last few years and have been shown to be so effective in treating patients that they are now recognized therapies in the UK's National Health Service, and doctors can prescribe a six-week mindfulness course to their patients.

SEEING THROUGH THE ILLUSION

In my experience, most of our thoughts aren't real. Most of the restrictive stories (or thoughts) we tell ourselves are just an illusion, hand-me-down beliefs we've picked up from other people or places along the way. Often we think the same thoughts over and over again so many times that they feel so real and this internal dialogue is normal. For most of us the mind is stuck in tape loop, on autopilot, and the story we have about life and who we are becomes a movie repeating subconsciously in the back of our minds.

You see, life is a bit like being in the cinema, scoffing popcorn as we watch a movie and react to what we see on the screen. But this particular movie is playing inside your head! That's great if your head is full of positive, joyful scenes or you've trained your mind to see the goodness in life and in yourself, but not so great if you're watching some old VHS that has been in your head for a very long time and is covered in cobwebs! Or you're glued to a drama that never ends, or fixated to some horror film that scares the sh#t out of you!

Most people feel trapped by their minds because their heads are filled with so many useless and unreal stories of fear, limitation, judgement and negativity. For some, it's depression, anger, stress, addiction, frustration or sadness that steals their happiness, and in the end what they see on the screen of their minds becomes their baseline and identity for life. It becomes normal to think such thoughts and you'll never talk them out of it. But it's only a movie they are playing out in their head. It's not real! At any given time you can change any story or thought patterns. When you do, your mind becomes a playground of possibilities!

Whatever the movie playing in your mind, if the story is not serving your purpose or taking you closer towards your goals you might as well walk out of the cinema! More to the point, you can choose what film you want to watch and be the director of your own movie. In Chapter 3 we'll be grabbing some popcorn (salted or sweet, your choice) and learning how to wire the best movie ever into your subconscious mind so you can create the best life yet! But for now we need to uncover the old script that's got stuck in a loop and is producing negative thought patterns!

EARLY SCRIPTS

We all have a script and story lodged inside our heads that we tell ourselves every day and that determines how we think and act in the world. We might not hear it out loud, but it's firmly wired inside our brains and it creates the reality we live in. We learn our early thoughts and stories from our parents, our peers, our culture, and the place we were born into. For instance, your dad might have told you to work hard for a living, money is tight, rich people are ruthless and so now you hate money, work hard to get by and have a poor relationship with your finances. Or your mum might have snapped at you as a child because you were always in the way, criticized your looks, so now you feel you need loads of make-up to look good and have low self-esteem or lack confidence. Or the kids at school made fun out of your appearance and size, or the media around you made you feel different because of the colour of your skin, your culture or the way you looked and now you feel odd, an outcast or like there's something wrong with you. Of course, all of our early teachings can have the complete opposite effect too! Either way, whatever story we picked up as kids, chances are it is still firmly wired into our heads.

We are all living inside our heads and creating life from within. The story you keep telling yourself about life is creating your life and who you become in the future. The thing is most of this happens subconsciously, so you might not even hear your story and the deepest thoughts that drive your actions. You have to become like a ninja and shake your mind as you dig deep! Either way – you'll be experiencing the consequences of your thoughts every day of your life until you do so. Keep telling yourself you're worthy of success then you'll create it. Devalue yourself and think you'll never succeed and you'll fail. Keep telling yourself how beautiful you are and how good you look and you'll have high self-esteem and love the person staring back at you in the mirror. Beat yourself up daily and judge your looks constantly and you'll hate yourself and feel uncomfortable in your own skin. Remember, whatever you think, you become! If you want more from life then you need to choose your thoughts wisely and challenge the unhelpful thoughts one by one as you begin to change your story!

If you want a better life, then you need to change the script inside your head!

Each time I uncovered a limiting belief or story, I noticed a number of things. First, they weren't even my beliefs or thoughts but ones I'd picked up along the way. Second, I could choose new and empowering thoughts and beliefs and create a new story in my head and when I repeated them daily my outlook on life changed and life transformed. Third, I could tell myself any story I wanted, because there are no rules to thinking – we all make it up as we go along, so why not make it epic? Before I knew it, I was living out the story I wired inside my brain!

....

⊕ What's your story?

Grab a pen and your journal and turn to the first blank page. Don't worry, no one will see what you write. This is between you and you! Be honest with yourself when you answer the statements below, but don't make it too complicated or get bogged down in the detail. No essays needed here! Literally let your mind and pen do all the work and write down every story that you've been telling yourself over the years. Remember not to judge yourself or blame others when you uncover your stories. This is about waking up and we wake up by taking full responsibility!

Here are a few thoughts to get you started:

* My current story about money is . . .
* My current story about a relationship is . . .
* My current story about food is . . .
* My current story about my parents/family/children is . . .
* My current story about myself is . . .
* My current story about love is . . .
* My current story about success is . . .
* My current story about my health is . . .
* My current story about my life is . . .

When you see your thoughts and beliefs staring back at you, a couple of things might happen. You might feel exposed, confused, frustrated or even pissed off because you see how and why life might not be working out how you wanted it! But just read through what you've written without any judgement and answer the following questions for each one:

* How has the story you've been telling yourself affected your life?

* How has the story you've been telling yourself affected your success?

* How has the story you've been telling yourself affected how you feel?

You'll notice that the story you've written down is also the life you have created, because what you think in your mind is how you show up in the world. Not rocket science, I know. But now ask yourself for each statement:

* Is this story true?

* If it is true, how is it true?

* Why is it true?

* And where or from whom did you learn this story?

Keep asking yourself, 'Is it true?' You'll be surprised at what you might find. When you wake up to the fact that your stories are an illusion and that you can change them, it feels so light and refreshing!

At first, waking up to your story might make you feel like you're going insane and thinking more negatively. Don't panic, this is part of the process – this noise has always been going on inside your head at a subconscious level, it's just now you've become aware of it. All you're doing is becoming more aware of your negative loops, so that you can choose to challenge them and interrupt the old script that's holding you back.

Personally, whenever I set myself a big goal, whether it's to write a book, be a public speaker or make more money, I notice my monkey mind rear up and my fearful or doubtful voice might tell me I'm not good enough or try to talk me out of it. I know, however, that this is just some old wiring I picked up along the way and that the thoughts are bullsh#t so I've learnt to challenge them and choose new ones! Never let your negative thoughts hold you back or stop you from taking action. Charge towards your goals and challenge your thoughts!

TRANSFORMING YOUR OLD STORY

The more you become aware of your old story and the script inside your head (the thoughts you often tell yourself), the easier it is to change any area of your life. You will learn in Chapter 4 that change is a crucial element of a happy and successful life, but no change will last or stick if you haven't transformed your old story first. When you start to uncover your old story, you'll begin to recognize the negative self-talk a lot more. You'll start to hear your self-criticism, judgements and any harsh language you might use against yourself. For instance, you might hear you're not smart enough, clever enough, thin enough or you're unlovable, unlucky, broken, a failure or weird! Whatever you hear, remember it's just a story. Like builders working on a derelict site, we need to remove the rubble and dig new foundations before we can start building a huge skyscraper that stands tall and confident!

When you know how to interrupt your old movie, you can mentally walk out of the cinema in your head and start to engineer your mind into a more peaceful and positive place. The more you interrupt the old damaging story and tell yourself about what's possible and what's not, the easier it becomes to recognize your true potential and know what you need to do next to create one epic life!

Now for the fun part!

....

⊕ Write a new script

Turn to a fresh page and start writing down a new story about life, yourself and your future, one that empowers you, excites you, makes you feel great about yourself and inspires you into action! For example:

* I choose my new story about money to be ...
* I choose my new story about relationships to be ...
* I choose my new story about health to be ...

Keep writing out new empowering statements and create the best story you could ever imagine. The more often you tell yourself this new story, the quicker it will become a reality.

....

It wasn't until I was locked up in prison that I started to hear the story I was telling myself. I wasn't good enough. A waste of space. A failure. A huge mistake. My story had me caught deep in victim mentality. That story was never going to get me anywhere in life so I needed to shift it, but first I had to understand it. If you want something new to show up in your life but keep telling yourself the old story, then life will be like cycling up hill with the brakes on. You'll get nowhere fast!

In the next chapter, you'll learn a powerful technique to hardwire a new story into your mind and turn it into a reality, but for now just write it down. What story would you would rather hear inside your head than the one you've been telling yourself? What do you really want from life?

Tattoo it on your mind, ignite it in your spirit and never give up! I've seem some radical changes in my clients' lives, sometimes in as little as a month, when they woke up to their limiting story and rewired a new one inside their heads.

THINK POSITIVE THOUGHTS

Positive people send out a different vibration to the universe because their thoughts are more creative and powerful. In Chapter 3 we'll be looking at the Law of Attraction and how 'like attracts like' but I'm sure you've experienced it many times. For example, think about being around someone, perhaps a friend or relative, who always seems to drain the life out of you? Chances are they're using negative words and expressing judgements that indicates their minds are filled with negative thoughts. Those who moan and groan the most usually have the biggest battles going on inside their heads.

From now on, pay attention to how you think and feel when you walk away from a conversation. Do you feel light and refreshed or a bit heavy and negative? Our thinking is so powerful that it can affect others just as much as it affects us. Always look for the good in others and every situation and send out positive thoughts. If you always like to be right, play judge and jury over others, or find yourself belittling others, then it's likely that your ego has taken over and you need to get more control over the monkey mind.

I've found that the only way to see positive results in life is to start by creating a positive projection, a brighter outlook, when we look out into the world. Choose to see the best in people, go beyond their patterns, the colour of their skin, size, attitudes and behaviours, and connect to the real magic inside them. After all, it's the same for all of us – especially when it comes to judging yourself. Be kind and gentle with your thoughts and the words you use to talk to yourself.

The only way to think positive is to choose to think positive! Perhaps that's stating the obvious, but, honestly, how long do you spend each day talking and thinking positively to yourself? I'm guessing not that long. So now you have some new stories (from the previous exercise) about the life you want to live and how you want to feel, spend at least five minutes each day saying these new sentences. It might seem almost too simple, but repetition is the key to rewiring a more positive script in your mind. Tell yourself your new story often enough and it will literally uproot the old one and replace it with your new one. You might even want to record your statements on your phone and computer, stick your headphones in and have your new script loop round for about 30 minutes. After about five minutes, your mind goes into a hypnotic trance as the new, more positive thoughts hardwire into your brain. Epic!

....

⊕ Get down and Get Zen

Getting silent and clearing your mind is key if you want quieter thoughts and more peace. I've been studying meditation for almost a decade and the technique below is a simple yet powerful way to help you reconnect to the magic and go way beyond your thoughts and the story in your mind. Find time every day for this exercise and practise, practise, practise. You might want to record this meditation so you can play it back while you get Zen or head over to www.wakethefckup.com to download a free recording of the above meditation to help you engineer your mind.

Find a quiet place where you won't be disturbed. Get comfy in a chair and close your eyes. Sit tall with an erect spine but not so rigid that you're uncomfortable. Begin by focusing on your breath. Take slow, deep breaths in and out through your nose. Feel your body start to relax, let go of any tension, and just allow your muscles to relax and chill.

Now I want you to imagine following the breath in your body. As you breathe in through your nose, follow your breath as it travel inwards through your nostrils. Then follow the air into the back of your throat, down into your lungs and deep down into your chest. As you breathe out, breathe out any stress, tension or worry with it. Simply let go!

On your next in-breath, follow your breath again and inhale the fresh air and the lightness from life, but this time travel down deeper into your chest and into the pit of your stomach and keep your focus and attention here, just below your belly button area, in the centre of your core. Let's take a body scan to relax even more.

Focus on your left hip and imagine feeling the energy there. Now take that energy down your left leg towards your left foot. Breathe in and out and let your left leg relax as you focus on your left foot. When you're ready, take your attention back up your left leg and then do the same on your right leg. Start at your hip and follow the energy down your right leg to your right foot and relax. Keep breathing in and out.

When you're ready, bring all that energy back up your right leg and return your focus to your centre, just below your belly button again. Notice how balanced and grounded you feel. Do your legs feel heavy, relaxed or tingling with energy compared to the rest of your body?

Now let's do the same relaxation technique with your arms.
Focus on your left shoulder and bring your attention to the
energy in your left shoulder and slowly come down your left
arm to your left hand. Feel the energy in your left hand and
relax. Sink deeper and deeper with every breath. After three
to five breaths, come back up your left forearm, to your left
elbow back to your left shoulder. Now go across your chest to
you right shoulder and let's do the same again. Slowly come
down your right arm, towards your right elbow and down your
right forearm. This time bring your energy and awareness to
the inside of your right hand. Feel the energy in the palm of
your hand. It might tingle or feel like pins and needles. Just
keep your attention inside your right hand and breathe in and
out. After a few breaths come back up your right forearm, to
your right elbow and back to your right shoulder. Notice how
relaxed your body feels.

Now the body is relaxed, bring your focus and attention
up to your head and focus on your mind. Begin to observe
your thoughts. Are you thinking about what you had for dinner,
what's on TV tonight, where you're going on holiday next
year, or who screwed you over five years ago. Pay attention to
where your thoughts are trying to lead you. Chances are they
are never in the now, in the moment or in the bliss! The mind
simply loves distraction and taking us away from the now. Be
strong and gentle with your mind, you want to take control but
in a kind way.

You might find the mind is a little calmer now your body is
more relaxed or it might be busier – and that's cool too – just
watch your thoughts whizzing around and focus on your breath.

Let your shoulders really relax and let go of any tension. Let your back and spine relax too, and when you feel calm begin to observe your mind by watching your thoughts. Choose not to follow them, just watch them come and go.

The key to meditation is to watch your mind without any labels, criticisms or judgements. Something many of us struggle with. Just observe any thoughts that pop into your mind and imagine they are not yours. Choose not to follow them, just watch them without any judgement. You might not be able to stop them from flashing into your head so use this Buddhist mantra and silently say to yourself, 'I'm breathing in' on every in-breath and 'I'm breathing out' on every out-breath.

When you notice your mind wandering, as it certainly will, or you catch yourself being taken down a stream of thoughts, or having a full-blown conversation with yourself, just bring your attention back to your breath. Remind yourself that you are just 'breathing in' and 'breathing out'.

For the next 10–20 minutes, or as long as it feels comfortable, observe every thought, sensation or feeling that arises within you but do your best not to attach to them. Rather than react and follow every distraction, stay still and breathe in and out. You'll notice that the calmer your mind is the calmer your body will be and vice versa. Remember never to judge any thought that pops into your mind, even if you don't like it. Just witness the busy-ness of your mind.

THE SPACE IN BETWEEN

The purpose of meditation and focusing on your breath is to end up in between your thoughts. By this I mean the emptiness, the clear, still space where thoughts do not exist. When you practise staying in the space in-between, your thoughts then act as a guide to let you know that you are not in the stillness (the now). Each time you catch yourself thinking, remind yourself it's not real and choose to live in the space between, breathing in and out.

The mind never stops thinking, but meditation and focusing on our breath, can help us separate from the madness and create a little place of calm. For me, living more mindfully and practising meditation has been the key to my transformation. It has helped me totally transform my old story about life and who I thought I was in the world. Not only this, but living more consciously has allowed me to observe my actions and behaviours, connect more deeply and tap into so much more magic in life. Hands down, the 'Get down and Get Zen' meditation could be the best thing you ever do!

Like anything, you must do it regularly. I'd suggest doing it either first thing in the morning or last thing at night for at least 10 to 20 minutes. If you really want to create a calm and peaceful mind and change your story about any area of your life, then mindfulness and meditation are the way forward! According to the teachings of the Buddha (some wise dude who woke up 2,500 years ago), regular mindfulness and meditation can lead to enlightenment and release us from all problems and suffering. Not bad!

CHAPTER 2

ENGINEERING YOUR CONSCIOUSNESS

'MANY PEOPLE ARE ALIVE BUT DON'T TOUCH THE MIRACLE OF BEING ALIVE.'

Thich Nhat Hanh

17 AUGUST 2003

It turned out that prison was the best thing that ever happened to me. Forced to live on the inside, I finally stopped and reconnected to myself. The time away gave me a break from the madness and the crazy life I'd led in Carshalton. I was no Tony Montana, but I sold a few bars of coke, kilos of skunk and moved thousands of pills each month. But all the chasing around Carshalton for my money, getting high and dodging dealers did my head in. Prison on the new wing was like a mini retreat. I knew loads of the local lads, smoked puff, hit the weights, played football, drank hooch and got paid to mop the landings, which got me out of my cell more.

Locked behind bars, I was about to find something where I least expected to . . . in a small paperback book in the prison library. I was in the library doing a deal, waiting for another inmate, walking up and down the aisles, looking shady and suspicious, when a book just fell to the floor and landed by my feet. Looking left and right to see if someone was messing with me, I slowly bent down to pick it up. It felt strange, I'd never read a book before, but I was drawn to read the front cover – *Moment by Moment* by Jerry Braza, a book about mindfulness and meditation.

At the time, I wasn't interested in mindfulness or slowing down. I was a drug dealer up to no good. My upbringing consisted of racist conditioning, listening to Dad's colourful stories about football hooliganism and getting wrecked! Love and connection were not regular topics of conversation – funny that! At first, I thought the book was about religion, the God squad or some flower-power bullsh#t trying to preach to me. Spirituality never crossed my mind. I was too busy chasing my tail and getting hooked on the devil's drug. I was never going to sit still and meditate, because my head was all over the place. I was a slave to my thoughts. They criticized me, condemned me and judged me daily. And I certainly didn't believe in anything cosmic in the sky!

Yet banged up in prison with nowhere to go, holding the book in my hands I felt safe. Like it was meant to be. Then that same voice I'd heard when I was parked up in my Fiat Bravo spoke, '*Read it, Brett!*'

F#ck it, I had nothing to lose so I began reading the blurb on the back and it seemed easy enough – common sense, even. Just breathe in and out and slow down. Become mindful of your thoughts and take time to connect. '*A bit too simple,*' I thought! But I knew it wasn't that easy because I wasn't in control of my life or my thoughts, they controlled me.

Flicking through the pages, I somehow felt a sense of peace and calm. Something inside me was stirring, urging me to read the rest of the book. The inner voice was getting louder. Sounds odd, but holding the book in my hands I felt a sense of freedom. For a moment, being locked away in **HMP** *High Down* didn't bother me any more, the negative voice usually talking to me inside my head faded away and I felt connected to something bigger. '*Maybe this can sort my life out!*' I thought as I stuffed the book down my tracksuit bottoms and walked out of the library.

Back in my dingy cell, I immersed myself in the book and read it every night. After a few weeks, things looked brighter.

Despite the cynical and judgemental voice piping up every now and then saying, '*What the f#ck are you doing Brett, finding God?*', I chose to read every word of *Moment by Moment* twice over and practised the simple exercises. I noticed how my thoughts seemed to be separating from me and it was clear to see my negative thoughts were playing on a tape loop in my mind and weren't really me and that I was more than the bunch of negative beliefs that had been conditioned in my head.

Jerry Braza's book made perfect sense to me. It helped me slow down and tune out of the negative loops in my head and wake up to my harmful patterns. I practised mindfulness when mopping the wing, I connected to the air when they let us out to play football and I meditated most nights. The more I separated from my thoughts, the more I saw that I was a slave to my ego and that the real prison was the cage in between my ears. My mind had taken me hostage and I'd never noticed before. I knew if my ego stayed in charge and I didn't take control of my thoughts, then I'd be in for a life sentence of more of the same!

CONSCIOUSNESS: WHEN YOUR WAKE-UP CALL STARTS RINGING!

Consciousness is often described as the energy inside us and all around us – the invisible force that bonds the universe together and holds our bodies together. We can't see it but we know it's there and we feel it when we feel alive. Science has proved that everything is energy, energy vibrating at very, very fast speeds. From the book you're holding in your hands to the breakfast you ate this morning, the plane in the sky right down to every cell and tiny atom within your body, everything is spinning and vibrating with pure energy like mini-tornados! Even down to the feelings that take over your body and the thoughts that swirl around inside your mind, they too have an energetic and electrical charge!

When we clear our minds, separate from the ego and the negative thoughts lodged inside our heads, we can connect to this energy and engineer a more conscious way of life. And that, in a nutshell, is what engineering consciousness is all about: expanding your mind, reconnecting to the bliss, learning to tune into the real you, rather than the ego, so you can shift your life to the next level.

The great thing about expanding your levels of consciousness is that you keep learning more about yourself, you grow and are able to zoom out and take a look at your life from a higher perspective – which means you can view your negative thoughts, unwanted patterns and destructive behaviours from a higher place. And you'll find that it's this higher view, this ability to separate from your thoughts, that gives you the advantage in breaking your old patterns, challenging your negative thoughts and really stepping into the now.

Nowness is where the bliss is found, because you can't feel happy or at peace when you're worrying about the past or stressing about the future. When we live in any time zone other than the now, we miss life itself – the real-time moment. When we go about our daily lives being conscious of the present moment, we tune into the magic and notice that life is a lot deeper and the moments become a lot richer. You engage and connect with life around you with more awareness and wake up to the universe within.

The more you engineer consciousness, the louder your inner voice becomes and it guides you towards better outcomes in your life. Everything that happens in your life is a reflection of your levels of consciousness. The money you earn, where you live, the people you know and the love you feel right now – everything boils down to your levels of consciousness. When you learn how to reconnect and engineer consciousness, you'll find that new thoughts pop into your head. Visions flash into your mind. Ideas wake you up and excite you. But, best of all, you tap into a natural high and buzz for life! Life glows again, you feel alive, nature vibrates, your love and connections become deeper and opportunities become greater.

Admittedly, it took me a while to access that special place and stay there, and I'm still learning just like everybody else, but focusing on my breath, challenging my thoughts and connecting to that inner voice empowered me and gave me control over my actions.

That itch you feel inside you, or that yearning to live a better life, is your consciousness calling you to the next level. It wants you to evolve! Once you acknowledge your inner voice, reconnect to it and listen to its guidance, you'll find yourself naturally breaking negative patterns, understanding who you really are at a deeper level and connecting to more bliss more habitually.

BEING CUT OFF FROM CONSCIOUSNESS

The trouble is that many people are so used to living inside their heads, ruled by their ego and their negative thoughts, that they dismiss consciousness as 'bonkers'. What they don't see is that they are so enslaved by the thoughts in their heads, that they've lost that special connection to life and this epic adventure. Being pushed around by society, the news and the fear in the media, their lives have become hard, tiresome and a struggle. Living from one drama to the next, working just to pay bills, drifting from one distraction to another.

Society and the media pile on the pressure to earn more, consume more, while also subliminally sending us the message that we won't fit in unless we follow the crowd, stay in line or keep up with the rest of the herd! Huge organizations rake in the profits from our stress – why should they care if it's making us sick? And sneaky marketers and tabloid papers feed off our emotional turmoil. No wonder so many people feel so disconnected and believe they are a sum total of their negative thoughts, guilty pleasures and habitual patterns.

We get so caught up in the 9 to 5 illusion that we lose sight of the inner connection that we all deeply crave. In other words, we're so busy living external lives that we forget to connect to the now and actually live life as it happens or look within to find our inner strength, internal peace and true wealth. When we follow the crowd, we simply forget who we are and can spend a whole lifetime feeling disconnected, frustrated and confused. We zone out, indulge, become lazy and eventually, over time, can feel cut off from the zest of life. Chances are most people won't admit this, they're way too busy being busy. And, perhaps, when they do find a moment to pay attention to how they really feel and the thoughts they really think, they do their best to ignore them, block them out and pay no attention to their wake-up call. This is why so many people have lost their spark and feel cut off and disconnected. Engineer consciousness and you'll reignite that inner spark!

The truth is that we never lose this connection to the bliss. It's always here and never leaves us. In fact, life is constantly doing its best to help us reconnect and remind us to slow down. From the beauty in a flower, to the joy and passion in a child's eyes, a leaf falling from a tree or the excitement we feel when we express ourselves and tap into our creativity. The gut instinct we feel, the intuition we have, the spontaneity that wants us to be curious and live in the moment. These inner feelings and miracles of creation can help us find our zest for life, but only if we stop to pay attention to them. Only if we tap into them and ignite them. This is why it is so important to slow down and reconnect to the moment, because that's when we hear the inner knocking and feel the itch inside our hearts.

What ignites you?

Now more than ever before is the time to look within and reignite your inner spark. To become more mindful of the connection with your children, to follow your dreams, ignite your passions and express your creativity. Now is the time to really find your purpose in life and live with more peace and passion! Because, let's face it, most people are running on empty, they look beat and lost, and they are not living one epic adventure. The world needs people to step it up and wake up!

As I said earlier, we're never actually cut off from the magic, our inner spark can never die, but when life gets busy and the ego takes over, the mind gets foggy and the magic definitely fades. So I want you to spend a few minutes thinking of all the things that light you up, bring you back to life and into the moment, lift your spirits and really get your juices flowing. Think about what makes you feel alive and present. When do you feel really high, happy and connected?

It might be when you dance or sing in the shower, play football with the lads, paint a picture or cuddle your child, express your creativity, give back, raise money for charity or tune into nature, or have the family round for a roast. Write down a list of the things that make you feel alive and connected to the joy of life.

⊙ What cuts you off?

Now take a look at all the negative crap that cuts you off from the moment. Turn to a new page and write a list of the things that leave you feeling sh#tty, down in the dumps, or disconnected. You know – the stuff you zone out to, indulge in and wish you'd never done it after you did it! For example, your list might include some or all of the following:

* Taking drugs
* Using pornography
* Drinking alcohol
* Binge eating
* Meaningless sex
* Zoning out to TV and box sets
* Gossiping and bitching
* Spending money you don't have
* Consuming stuff to feel good

Think about what you indulge in and how it makes you feel afterwards. Do these things add more happiness and pleasure to your life or do you enjoy the moment of gratification only to find it leaves you feeling crappy, guilty, disconnected or even ashamed? Albert Einstein described insanity as 'doing the same thing over and over again and expecting different results'. If you want an epic life with more energy and abundance, then you need to let go of the sh#t that drains you!

You are in charge of your inner spark. You, and only you, can light it up!

Either you're kindling your spark by doing positive things that feed it and keep it alive or it's disappearing because you're going through the motions, your ego has taken you hostage and you're repeating unwanted patterns that then fuel negative thoughts and feelings. As you know, I've been there myself, so you're in good company. Following the crowd, doing stuff because it's socially acceptable, and, nowadays, expected, can only ever create a baseline of misery and sameness, not bliss!

From now on, pay close attention to your behaviours. Before you indulge in something that leaves you feeling disconnected afterwards, zoom out and visualize how you'll think and feel after you've done it. Then ask, 'Is it worth it, do I really want to feel that way afterwards?' If you feel disconnected and disassociated from the life you want to be living and how you really want to feel, then work on cutting out the crap and adding more of the stuff that makes you feel connected. Think about the list that brings you more joy and connects you more deeply to life and do more of that more often!

I'm not saying you need to become a saint! It's fine to watch a movie or have a good chin-wag with your friends, but if it leaves you feeling cut off or drains your energy, you need to work out whether spending three hours a night watching TV, acting out, getting drunk or gossiping with friends is really adding any value to your life.

TUNING INTO THE BLISS – CONSCIOUSNESS!

I truly believe that life is a celebration and it can be experienced blissfully when we step into the now and let go of all the illusions and distractions that take us away from the moment and cut us off from consciousness. When you step into the now, you start to experience a deeper feeling of joy and connection with the world around you and inside you. You feel the energy buzzing through your body. Your mind becomes so clear and free. When you practise living in the now, in the space in between your thoughts and feelings, you'll also recognize that there are no negative thoughts, critical judgements or labels – just pure oneness with life.

I'm sure you've felt this connection before, perhaps in a moment of peace and stillness, when you were out in nature, stroking your pet or spending time with your children, or really connected with your lover. Life seemed to make more sense, you felt free, alive and connected, and everything seemed quieter and more peaceful. That was you reconnecting to the bliss!

Scientists, spiritual teachers, physicists and philosophers have spent years debating this mystery that is consciousness, but in all that time they've only scratched the surface. Most experts, including Einstein, simply admit there is something that connects everything in this universe together and that same something is running through each and every one of us. Is it the spirit? Is it the soul? Who knows? I'm not here to prove God, energy, consciousness or spirit exists. If Mr Einstein can't explain it, I doubt this cheeky chap will! I think labels take us away from the magic, even the term I'm using, 'consciousness', is just a word for our brains to logically grasp. It doesn't really do the magic any justice.

Truth is, you don't need to be a scientist, a cheeky chap or a guru to understand consciousness. Think about it, you don't need to believe in gravity to know that if you or I jump off a tower block then it's game over. You know gravity exists, it's a given. You also know that the stars twinkle high up in the night sky and the sun will rise tomorrow.

At some point in your life, it's likely that you felt connected to that special something, something phenomenal within you, but perhaps you just can't put your finger on it or never really thought about it. Maybe you haven't felt it for some time, but remember feeling that way when you were a free-spirited child. Doesn't that mean it's still within you? And don't you think it's magical that something wakes us up every day? That subconsciously we breathe over 20,000 breaths each day? That, while the blood pumps through our bodies, thoughts are continuously swirling around inside our heads, and sometimes we feel energized and connected to the bliss? When you think about it, doesn't it seem obvious that something unexplainable is living inside each and every one of us?

....

⊙ Experiencing consciousness

Try this. Raise both your hands out in front of you to chest height. Stick both your middle fingers up and connect them together so they are touching one another fingertip to fingertip. For the next 60 seconds just breathe in and out gently and bring your awareness and attention to where your index fingers are connecting. Feel the blood pumping through your fingers, and feel the energy and consciousness keeping you alive. You can stay here for as long as you like, do this on the train, interrupt your ego when it gets too busy, or like me do it for fun to remind

you how much of a miracle you really are and how something wonderful is keeping you alive. Close your eyes for a deeper experience – it's epic!

....

Just because energy and consciousness are invisible like gravity doesn't mean they don't exist! Like the size of the universe, consciousness goes way beyond what we can ever grasp within our limited minds or see with the human eye. But connecting to this universal magic and investigating this peculiar feeling within you is the key to waking up!

Engineering your consciousness is as simple as recharging your phone.

Consciousness is our most natural state – before the ego developed (our thoughts and our identity) and before our parents, our environment and the system conditioned us, we lived in this blissful state more often. Think about the last baby you saw in a coffee shop or smiled at, I'm guessing that they looked totally connected to the joy. They don't beat themselves up, have limiting thoughts or worry about money, they're just being and feeling connected to the moment. The problem many people face is that life is getting busier and faster, and we grow up in a world that takes us away from the bliss. Over time we forget what it used to feel like and that we still have this magic inside us. For some it feels as though it has disappeared or was never there. So let's take a few moments to enter the now and remember what that connection feels like.

•••

⊕ Stepping into the now

Take a few deep breaths and spend a few minutes just focusing on the movement of your breath as you inhale and exhale. Now, look at the dot in the centre of the circle below and keep focusing on it for about 30 seconds.

Chill out, relax and follow your breath in and out before asking:

* What does it feel like to be me staring at the dot?
* Who's inside me staring at the dot?

You may feel as though you're looking at the dot through a window or inside a body looking out through a set of eyeballs. I know, state the obvious! But you may experience some stillness and calmness as you enter the now. You may feel more present or in the moment. That strange feeling is often described as consciousness – it's when you separate from your ego and the repetitive self-talk and rise above your negative thoughts so you can engage with life more deeply. You step into the nowness of life.

From here on, for the rest of your life, I want you to practise staying in this still space in between your thoughts and feelings as much as you can, because this is how you engineer an amazing life and create so much freedom from negative thoughts and heavy feelings! You can do it when you're washing up by focusing on the dishes, the water, the soap bubbles; in the shower when the water splashes over your head; or when you're talking to a friend but focusing on your breath and the person in front of you. When you do this and live in the now, there's no judgements or negativity, just observation, clarity and awareness. Try it when you're next walking down the road, focus on your breath and on each step, feel the connection to the ground and how your foot connects to the earth. You can even do it while you're reading this book. Really engage and connect to each word you're reading right now and tune out of your thoughts by staying in the now.

The more often you engineer this state, the quieter your mind will become and the freer you'll feel. Over time, consciousness will become automatic and your most natural state of being.

Do it again. Just stare at the dot for a few moments, become aware of this feeling and stay present, in the here and now and feel it! If your inner voice pipes up or your thoughts try to take you away from the moment, bring your attention back to your breath, choose not to follow your thoughts and other distractions, don't judge them – simply focus on the dot.

⊙ Tuning into Consciousness

To take this technique one step further, go to the nearest window, open it and look outside. Spend a few minutes just observing and watching life. Look at any buildings, trees or birds, and any people walking past. Watch anything that takes your interest and zone out of your head and tune into consciousness.

When you're first starting to connect like this, you may find it easier to observe the natural world rather than people, because we don't tend to judge plants and animals the same way we do people. I like to stare at trees, because they have such an incredible energy consciousness!

Now, just as you did in the previous exercise, focus on one object intently for about 30 seconds, then ask:

* What does it feel like to be alive right now?

* How do I feel inside now I'm aware of my awareness?

Simply keep looking. Now take your awareness to your body, and ask:

* Do I feel warm or cold?

* Can I feel my heart beating or my pulse pumping?

* How does it feel to be the witness of my life?

Now take your awareness outside of yourself. Imagine being whatever it is you're focusing on – whether that's a tree, a cloud or an animal – how does that feel? Imagine you've left your body and are floating outside, where are you now?

When I'm walking along the road, I often focus on a tree in front of me. When my thoughts pipe up, as they invariably do, I take my attention to my breath, then to the tree and remind myself I am not my thoughts. It's pure bliss! I take my attention outside of my body and focus on what's happening out there, right now. If I'm standing in a queue, I imagine removing myself from my body, my thoughts and my feelings and focus on my breath. I just breathe deeply and slowly, and imagine I'm floating outside of myself and stepping into the now, because doing this creates such a feeling of freedom, oneness and connection! It's like your mind stops thinking and your feelings disappear (don't worry, they come back soon as you enter your body again).

Try it again. Put the book down for a few moments and go on a little journey. Take a walk round the block or go and talk to someone and really stay present. Focus on your breath and connect to the now. Step outside of yourself, your thoughts and the need to think of a label for anything, just stay present and be. This is a great technique for when you're feeling stressed or when your mind gets busy, or you feel like you can't switch off your thoughts. With practice, your mind will naturally enter this state of freedom, so that you no longer aimlessly follow every thought or get caught up in every feeling that pops into your mind or body. Practising consciousness teaches you to just let them go, let them float away, and stay in the now!

....

Stepping into the now can make you feel excited that you're alive and you might even feel the hairs on your arms stand to attention when you feel this epic connection to life. You may begin to feel a child like excitement and enthusiasm for life, as a new, but strangely familiar, feeling starts to erupt within you. This feeling may have been dormant for many years, but once you ignite it, it rushes through your body and reminds you that you are here, alive in this moment, and having one of the best adventures of your life.

When you catch your thoughts or feelings trying to lead you astray, gently bring your attention back to your breath and what you're doing. In this way, you start bringing more awareness into your everyday experience and begin to create a more present way of being.

CONVERSATIONS WITH CONSCIOUSNESS

For years, great leaders and teachers such as Mahatma Gandhi and the Dalai Lama have suggested we look within and quiet the mind so we can pay more attention to our inner voice. It turns out that the more you tune out your old thought patterns and separate from your ego and connect to the now, the more you'll hear this inner voice. It seems to me this voice is always trying to direct our lives and connect with us, but we are often too busy, distracted by daily life and social demands.

I described at the start of the book how I was busy smoking crack when I head a voice telling me I would change my life and write a book; but I didn't have a clue where it came from. I just knew the voice sounded and felt so different from my usual self-talk. Now, after many years of conversations with this voice, I know it was consciousness trying to steer me in the right direction. It was knocking on the door and all I had to do was open up.

When you tune out of the rubbish inside your head and create inner stillness in your mind, your consciousness can connect with you. Most people ignore that voice or don't hear its positive messages, because their minds are filled with negativity and clutter. Consciousness is the voice that wants us to grow and evolve. But it's not just a voice, it's the inner tug you feel in your gut when you know something isn't right or when you know you're on to a good thing.

Consciousness is the voice in the back of your mind telling you which way to turn.

Without a shadow of a doubt, consciousness is trying to communicate with you and it can and will direct your life if you pay attention to it and tune in. You've probably heard it before, but mostly it goes unheard because the ego shouts louder. And because you know your ego so well and are used to its patterns, you ignore that inner voice. For example, you may have heard it warning you not to text an ex and you did text them but then regretted it, or had a gut feeling about a certain someone but ignored it only to find out they'd manipulated you or ripped you off. Or when your inner voice told you to go for something – a new job, a date or any kind of dream – and you went for it and nailed it and felt great because you listened to and trusted in yourself.

With hindsight we can always look back on our decisions and think to ourselves, why on Earth did I do that? We rarely pat ourselves on the back or congratulate ourselves for making the right choices and listening to our inner guide. But if we pay attention and investigate a little deeper, we'll probably discover there was some part of us that always knew that we had this voice steering our lives. Never ignore your inner voice, because it is doing its best to connect with you and make your life epic! The more you listen to this authentic voice inside you, the easier your life will become. In the end it's like you have the world's best coach guiding you, giving you the answers, and helping you move in the right direction. You can ask it questions before you make rash decisions, seek support and guidance and enjoy the amazing visions that flash into your mind!

Will the real Brett Moran please stand up . . .

When I first heard my consciousness talking to me, I thought I was really going crazy, and losing the plot. Hearing another voice in my mind wasn't what I was looking for. But this voice wasn't harsh and judgmental like the one I was used to. It was kinder, softer and far more positive! It took some time, but I realized it wanted me to succeed, that it had always been trying to steer me in the right direction and in the end it became my best friend and has now taken over from the negative side of my mind. At the start it was like I had two people living inside me. The little devil that wanted me to get bang on it, get drunk, sleep around, or do just about anything that made me feel cut off and like sh#t afterwards. But then this softer voice of inner truth and wisdom suggested I do things differently. And when I paid attention and took action, my life was radically transformed!

⊕ Engineering consciousness

Getting silent and engineering consciousness is like recharging your batteries and the following technique is a peaceful and powerful way to help you reconnect to the magic and go way beyond the ego in your mind. As with the meditation in Chapter 1, on page 24-8, you might want to record this meditation so you can play it back while you get Zen. Plus you can download your MP3 in your membership area at www.wakethefckup.com.

Find a quiet place where you won't be disturbed. Get comfy in a chair and close your eyes. Sit tall with an erect spine but not so rigid that you're uncomfortable. Begin by focusing on your breath. Take slow, deep breaths in and out through your nose. Feel your body start to relax, let go of any tension, and just allow your muscles to relax.

Now I want you to imagine following the breath in your body. As you breathe in through your nose, follow your breath as it travels inwards though your nostrils. Then follow the air into the back of your throat, down into your lungs and deep down into your chest. As you exhale, breathe out any stress, tension or worry too. Simply let go!

On your next in-breath, follow your breath again and breathe in the fresh air and the lightness from life, but this time travel down deeper into your chest and into the pit of your stomach and keep your focus and attention here, just below your belly button area, in the centre of your core.

Now, just as you did in the meditation in Chapter 1, scan your body, connect to your inner world and feel your energy rising.

Feeling relaxed in your body and mind, and with your eyes closed, take your attention to the centre of your forehead, just above your eyebrows. Look up towards your forehead and imagine someone has just come into the room and switched the lights on. Keep your eyes closed, but let the light into your mind. Sit here for a moment. Breathe and relax.

Imagine your body floating out through your forehead and travelling up into the sky. Go past the clouds, through the Earth's atmosphere and right out into deep space. Imagine how silent space is. Feel that silence and peacefulness. Imagine seeing millions of stars – they are so tiny that they look like grains of sand. As you float out deeper into space, you look down towards the Earth – you can barely see it. Our galaxy and planets are now like speck of dust. Go higher and deeper out into the cosmos. Breathe and relax. You are now connecting to your higher self, to consciousness.

Notice how free and connected you feel. Watch your ego and pay attention to your thoughts and let them float away one by one.

You can spend 5 or 50 minutes in this place. Download any information or wisdom you need. Ask questions and stay separate from your ego, connected to consciousness!

When you're ready to come back, slowly begin to descend towards Earth. See the planet getting bigger and bigger. As you get closer, see your body lying on the ground until you reach it and return to it through your forehead. Keep your eyes closed and travel back round your body. Feel the sea of consciousness swimming throughout your body connecting to every cell. When you are ready, slowly gently open your eyes.

You can ask consciousness anything. If you're looking for answers, just close your eyes and tune in. If you're stuck with a decision and not clear where to go, you can ask your higher self. Not sure of yourself or your future. Tune in and connect to your inner voice. The difference between consciousness and your current thoughts is that consciousness is the truth. It will never let you down. The ego is an illusion of 'who you are', and 'who you are meant to be', whereas your consciousness is pure and unconditional. It would never beat you up, judge you, criticize or belittle you. It simply wants you to feel great, enjoy life, succeed and evolve to the next level.

CHAPTER 3

ENGINEERING YOUR VISION

'YOU ONLY HAVE CONTROL OVER THREE THINGS IN YOUR LIFE – THE THOUGHTS YOU THINK, THE IMAGES YOU VISUALIZE, AND THE ACTIONS YOU TAKE.' Jack Canfield

21 OCTOBER 2003

One night I rolled over and gazed up at the drab ceiling. Tears welled up in my eyes and began to roll down my face because my mask had finally dropped. I was facing myself and it was hard. Looking within isn't easy, exposing the bullsh#t in my head felt raw! Becoming aware of my negative actions made me feel uncomfortable and I finally woke up to the fact that I had created the madness in my life. If I'm honest, I hated the person I'd become too! As I zoomed out and looked at myself and acknowledged how destructive my behaviours were hurting those who loved me, I felt empty and angry. I recognized how selfish my actions were and how I was letting my family down. Especially my baby, Ella!

Without thinking, I clasped my hands together, closed my eyes tight and prayed my little heart out! 'Look, if there's anything out there, if there's a God, a Buddha, anything, then please listen to me, I've had enough of this crazy sh#t. I've f#cked up big time and I want something different. I know I've done some bad stuff and I've hurt people, but I'm really sorry. I know I can change, just give me one more chance! Please help me out, I want out of this madness, I promise to do whatever it takes to be a better person. I'll do anything to change this life. Just show me a sign!'

Hitting rock bottom in prison was the best thing that ever happened to me. Instead of blaming others for my actions I understood that I was responsible: that my thoughts had created my actions and my actions had created my patterns. As I looked up to the sky, I asked for another shot at things.

To be honest, I didn't care if there was anyone or anything listening, it just felt good to get it off my chest, let go and get clear. 'I promise I will be a better person if you give me second chance.'

Now I was making deals with the big man upstairs!

I shut my eyes tighter and waited for an answer.

Nothing.

I prayed again. In case God, Buddha, the universe hadn't heard!

I opened my eyes, expecting the Dalai Lama to be sitting on the end of my bed in the lotus position sipping green tea. But nothing, there was no white light or spiritual glow!

'*What a waste of time*,' I thought as I rolled over and looked at the dull wall staring back at me.

Then all of a sudden, out of nowhere, a vision flashed into my mind as clear as daylight. Followed by feelings of hope, inspiration and relief. Something inside me ignited and for the first time ever my thoughts vanished!

Then, out of the blue, my imagination leaped into the future as if it had a mind of its own. I saw a vision and it felt so real and amazing. Whatever it was, this picture pierced through the usual noise in my mind and flashed right before my eyes. The insight looked really clear too, like I was watching a movie in my mind. It made perfect sense, I felt optimistic and excited about my future!

Then I heard that louder voice again, '*Brett, anything is possible. You can do this!*'

The image in my mind got bigger and brighter . . . It was Mum and Ella smiling and running around on a summer's day.

They looked so happy. I was in the picture too, but it wasn't the same me that was locked in prison dealing drugs, it was my future self. The sun was shining and now we were all running around on some field – totally in the now and connecting.

It was a simple vision, I know, but at the time, being stuck in prison, it was all I wanted. I wanted to be a great dad and cuddle my daughter. I wanted to make my mum proud of her only child. And in the vision I was doing that, I was clean, drug free and spending quality time with my family.

Over the following months, I took control of my imagination and used it to tune into that image most nights before I went to sleep. I made the picture in my mind more colourful and vibrant with positive feelings, and somehow I knew in my heart that one day it would be my reality. All I needed to do was take action and follow through! Peering into my destiny, I could see how well and happy I looked, just like I did when I was a kid before drugs came onto the scene. I was carefree and alive. I was happier than ever before. In fact, I was glowing. As I lay there visualizing being with Mum and Ella each night, I made a silent vow to the sky that I would do anything and everything to turn my vision into a reality!

VISION: USING YOUR IMAGINATION TO TRANSFORM YOUR DESTINY.

Using the power of your mind and imagination to create a clear, compelling and convincing vision for a life you want to experience in your future is one of the most universal tools for personal success. Seeing what you want in your mind's eye and leaping into your future gives you more energy, guidance and direction in life – yup, it's that simple. When you paint a clear picture of the life you want to live and who you want to become, your destiny pulls you towards that very path. On the other hand, without a vision we are lost, aimlessly plodding through life hoping some day things will change.

A vision means you are sensing your future before anyone else does – you are using your mind for what it was intended. When you align with your vision and make positive choices in life, you start to feel excited by the possibility of success, which in turn ignites more energy to turn your vision into a reality. You might find you wake up bright and early, full of energy and ready to get cracking, or stay awake late at night working on your vision because it makes your heart sing. Personally, I lose track of days when I am immersed in a project that lights me up. Time seems to disappear, I'm full of energy and I'm in the zone!

From that day in prison when I saw a vision of what my future could be like, I have been engineering my mind and continuing to create vision after vision to get what I want. I've pictured myself starring in films, getting book deals, getting out of thousands of pounds of debt, having thousands of pounds saved in the bank, living by the sea, doing my yoga training, having deeper and more meaningful relationships and meeting new friends. Many of those visions are now my reality and having a vision for my life has never yet let me down! Today I'm creating my future by visualizing ten years ahead. In this chapter, we'll explore the power of your imagination so you can create a destiny you love too!

Having a vision changes your perspective on life – you get more done, have clear direction, ignite more energy and feel excited about life!

We cannot hide from the future, we are all moving forwards. Some of us are hurtling with busy lives, missing the precious moments, while others are taking a more Zen approach and connecting to the now. But everyone on this planet is heading towards their destiny. So why not make it count, why not make it a future that excites you and gives you more passion, purpose and meaning? That way you're guaranteed a more joyful life when you get there, you have more focus in your life today and you have something greater to tune into when times get tricky!

....

 # THINK IT ENOUGH TIMES AND YOU'LL PROVE IT INTO REALITY!

The American spiritual leader Dr Leonard Orr described us as having two people living inside us, 'the Thinker' and 'the Prover', and said, 'what the Thinker thinks the Prover proves', meaning the thoughts and images we think in our minds create our world outside. We all live inside our own reality bubble: thinking and proving reality to ourselves. Even if it's not real! In other words, think your vision has already happened and the Prover will imprint it your mind and prove you right in a matter of time. By getting your inner Thinker and Prover on the same team, you can re-create your reality. If you think about what you really want in your life over and over again, then you'll prove it true before you know it!

....

BECOME A VISIONARY

Right, let's stop f#cking about and engineer the ultimate vision for your life! As you know, everything in this world is created twice, first in the mind, second in reality. Everything you see in the world started out as an idea, a vision in someone's imagination. Someone had to imagine trains hurtling around under the city for the Tube to become a reality in London, Gustave Eiffel had to visualize a metal tower standing tall in the Paris skyline, the Wright brothers dreamed about flying in the sky, while Mr Jobs imagined the smartphone sitting in your pocket and – BOOM – those visions became our reality! In the same way, if you want to change your life, make the world a better place or break negative patterns you have to see the outcome you want in your mind first so that you can create it, believe it and achieve it.

....

◎ **Where do you see yourself in 10 years?**
When you create a vision for your life be bold and brave, don't pussy foot around and wish for a few things to change, affirm to yourself that it's time to fix up and you want more from life, whether that be deeper relationships, stronger spiritual connection, more health, more wealth or more love. It takes the same amount of energy to dream small as it does to dream big.

By comparison, it takes more energy to be stuck in a rut, wishing your life was different. So turn to a new page in your journal and answer the following questions and really go to town. Let your imagination do the work and dream as you write out a few sentences for each question:

* In 10 years from now I want my relationships to be . . .

* In 10 years from now I want my health to be . . .

* In 10 years from now I want my love life to be . . .

* In 10 years from now I want my adventures to be . . .

* In 10 years from now I want my finances to be . . .

Now close your eyes and spend a few moments focusing on your breath and just letting your mind settle into the now. When you feel nice and zoned, think about where you want to be in the future and then spend some time drawing a mental picture of yourself as though you've already achieved it. Really imagine how it would feel to have it. How would you look, talk and act? What would people say to you, once you'd achieved it? What would you say to yourself, once you'd achieved it? How does living your vision make you feel?

Intentionally use the power of your imagination to see yourself enjoying what you want. Have fun, go wild and remember to keep focusing on what you want, not what you think is possible and achievable, and definitely not what you don't want – and we'll be looking at why this is important a little later in the chapter.

I'd suggest spending 10 minutes or so, perhaps when you wake up or last thing at night, seeing your vision. Later in this chapter, I'm going to share the visualization technique I've been using for years, and share with all my clients, so you can create one truly epic vision for your life. Plus I've created an MP3 in your membership site so you can download it and ignite the power of your imagination!

For me, seeing the vision of Ella and my mum in prison that night was like a breath of fresh air. But what's more my prison sentence got easier. My outlook changed and being banged up didn't seem so bad. In fact, I appreciated it for giving me the time to focus on how I would achieve my vision and create a new world with my family. I had to wake up to the life I didn't want so I could see the life I really wanted. So I planned my journey, wrote down my goals and sent letters to Ella and Mum telling them how I was going to sort my life out and change my ways. Even though the vision was still in my future, simply knowing where I was headed changed my energy and my outlook and made me feel more like I was in control of my life. I've since become the person I envisioned in prison and have spent countless sunny days running around on top of Old Sarum, a field in Salisbury, with Ella and my mum. I am literally living the vision I created a decade ago in a prison cell and it feels a billion times better than I ever imagined.

WHEN A VISION GOES WRONG

I know you're thinking, '*But it can't be that easy – just close your eyes and imagine your success!*' But you've probably seen the power of vision in action hundreds of times already. Perhaps you were thinking about a friend only to have them call you unexpectedly or bump into them in the street. Or you thought about a new car you wanted to buy and, boom, you saw the make and model everywhere. Or maybe it's been working in reverse. You keep worrying about the bills, have a vision of being stuck in debt and all the while more bills keep coming through the door, your car breaks down, your tooth cracks, or you lose your phone, and more money seems to be going out of your account rather than into it!

This happens because the power of your thoughts works both ways. Just as the size of the rock makes no difference to gravity – when you throw it out of the window, whatever size it is, it will always fall to the ground – your vision and thoughts are exactly the same. They don't care whether you think positive thoughts of success and abundance, or limiting thoughts of lack and worry, they simply give you what you think about and what you focus on!

Years ago, a few months before being arrested and sent to prison, I remember lying awake on my dad's settee feeling paranoid and alone. Dad was in Thailand and I had turned his flat into a drug den. The thoughts in my mind were driving me crazy! I had some cocaine stashed away and I couldn't stop snorting it. At one point, I lay on the settee because I thought my heart was going to explode and I remember begging something to stop me. I wished desperately that the police would boot down the door and lock me up to stop me taking drugs. I wanted to go to prison just so I could stop using. I know – crazy, right! But I'd lie awake all night visualizing the police arresting me and taking me away! As you know, I got sent down and it was literally months after I started thinking about going to prison.

If you can see it in your mind, then you can create it in your reality.

This is why the exercises in the last chapter were so important. You must uproot and weed out your old negative thoughts and challenge any negative stories that are stored deeply in your mind if you want to create more in your life, because those hidden beliefs will always attract what you think!

Meet Paul

As an aftercare leader, my role was to help addicts, ex-cons and homeless people reintegrate back into the community once they'd got clean. So I used a number of groups and clubs to entice them in, from DJ workshops to movie nights, fry-up Fridays to breakfast clubs. One night I chose to screen The Secret – a documentary about the Law of Attraction and bringing what you want towards you (if you haven't watched it, do it now – it's epic). So I brought a load of popcorn and fizzy drinks and invited a few of the lads. To be honest, I felt like one of them, only I did the paperwork at the end of the evening and they went off to score! After the film, Paul came up to me and I could tell he was inspired. 'I loved the film, Brett, it makes perfect sense and it's so simple. I'm going to think more positively and really focus on what I want.'

'Told ya' mate, it's all in the mind. You just got to think right and you'll change your entire life. So what do you want to create, Paul?' I asked, just as inspired as he was.

'Brett, I'm going to get clean, get a job and rebuild my life. That's all I really want. What about you?' he asked.

'Well, I'm clean so that's all sorted, but after watching Jack Canfield I've just decided I want to be in a film and share a message: If we can change mate, anyone can!'

So a few years later, I smashed it and ended up in a film with Jack. A few years after that, I had the privilege of meeting him in London with

Ella and shaking his hand. I wanted to thank him personally for sharing his message in The Secret, because it changed my attitude and really expanded my life and mind.

But the best bit about this story is how Paul turned his life around. He got clean, got a job, a house and a girlfriend and seems happier than ever!

Positive or negative, good or bad, you will always create and attract what you think about most. Whatever success looks like to you, it starts in your mind and how you choose to think and feel about it. If you want to lose weight and be healthy, then you need to see yourself looking sexy and trim, feeling lighter and weightless. If you want to fall madly in love with that special someone, then see yourself with Mr or Mrs Right, connecting deeply, sharing your values and living in your bubble and giving love. If you want more money in your bank account ,then give yourself permission to have it, think about the house you live in, the zeroes in your bank account, the new successful business you're going to start. When you deliberately set your intention and direct your thoughts, you expand your consciousness and it won't be long until you are pulled towards what you see in your mind's eye.

THE LAW OF ABUNDANCE

Without a shadow of doubt, we live in a world of plenty. There is a wealth of abundance all around us and within us 24/7. If you don't see it right now and feel it within you, then stick with me! When you think about it, there's lots of everything, wherever you look. First we have what I call 'Macro Abundance'. This is the immense magnitude of everything in life and the universe. For instance, try counting the leaves on a single tree, grains of sand on a beach, or the stars in the galaxy. It's impossible, and it never ends; it keeps on multiplying. In the last few years, millions more galaxies have been found and there's probably a million more to discover. It's the same with money, there are trillions being spent right now!

There is plenty of everything when we open our minds and see beyond our limiting beliefs.

The trouble is most people never spot the abundance of life or feel it. They feel lack and worry about scarcity or limitations and this fearful thinking keeps them stuck in old ways of thinking. I don't care what the collective beliefs are or what bulls#it they show us on the news, the truth is we live in a world of abundance, there's an endless supply to feed everyone on this planet. If we can pay footballers, musicians and actors millions for the entertainment, then I think we need to wake up! We just need to train our minds to see and feel the vibration of abundance within us. What you choose to do with your wealth is your business, but I'm guessing that if you are reading this book you've been doing a lot of good with it, so why not make millions and create a bigger change?

No matter what you think about, there is plenty of it and the first key to creating more abundance is tuning into it. When you start to see and feel the abundance in the world, you begin to experience this incredible feeling inside you and it rises up and changes your frequency. This is when life gets easier, because you stop worrying about lack and start focusing on plenty. You start feeling rich and wealthy from within. There have been times in my life when I couldn't even pay for my petrol, buy my daughter a present and had my phone cut off more times than I care to remember, but I was always able to laugh it off, see it as a lesson and tune into the abundance.

The second key to igniting that abundant feeling within you is what I call 'Micro Abundance'. I'm not sure how often you stop and think about your body and what lives inside you, but I do it on a daily basis and it triggers a rush of ecstasy inside me. Did you know we have over 37 trillion cells in the body and over 100 billion cells in the brain! Our veins and arteries can stretch over 100,000 miles and if you stretched out all of a human's blood vessels, they would be about 60,000 miles long. That's enough to go around the world twice over! If we spend just a few moments thinking about the abundance within us and all around us we unleash a peculiar feeling. I say peculiar, because no words can describe the sensation that swims through my body when I tap into this abundant feeling.

Abundance is everything and everywhere, inside you and out!

So why the anatomy lesson? Like attracts like and the way we create one epic adventure and get what we want from life is to dream it into reality with our minds then match it by vibrating at the highest frequency or, in other words, by focusing on positive feelings. If you walk around feeling stressed out, angry, depressed and desperate or thinking life is limited, then chances are you're never going to get what you really want because your thoughts and feelings will push it away, you'll repel your dreams and you'll live a life of lack. On the flip side, if you open your eyes and look for abundance everywhere and feel the rush swiming through every cell of your body, your outlook will change almost instantly. You'll activate your inner charge and attract new people, places and things into your life. Remember, everything is energy, including money, so if you want more then you need to match your vibration with it and see it as a form of exchange! Think the right thoughts and ignite the right feelings and cash will flow your way!

At the start of this year, I owed over £10,000 for a business that never even got off the ground. So I watched *The Secret* again, exchanged my thinking for more positive and constructive thoughts, and began to focus on abundance all around me to ignite that feeling in my being. Within six months, I'd paid the money back and saved more than £10,000 in the bank. I'm not a millionaire yet, and money is not my only goal in life, but it sure is better to feel in control of it and feel wealthy inside than to be a slave to it!

....

◉ Igniting that abundant feeling

For the next month, before you jump out of bed close your eyes for a moment and think about the abundance within you. Think about what you have just read, visualize the trillions of cells inside your body and feel the energy inside you. Then when you are out and about or commuting to work, train your brain to see abundance by counting everything all around you. For instance, try to count all the cars on the roads, the birds in the trees, or the people in the city. Simply spending a few minutes in the morning with your eyes closed thinking about abundance and activating that feeling will transform your life!

....

Transform your mindset from one of lack to one of plenty.

Seeing and feeling the Law of Attraction in action takes time. For example, it took me 30 days of meditating first thing in the morning on abundance and using the power of my imagination to activate this inner feeling. Now I can switch it on and off whenever I like! Soon as I wake up in the morning I do a meditation on abundance and think about what I want to create in my future. When I'm out walking a friend's dog, I'm counting the leaves on the trees, or when I look up at night I feel alive because I can't get my head around the vastness of space! Open your mind and practise this strategy today and you'll feel so amazing and your life will change faster!

CREATE A COMPELLING VISION FOR YOUR LIFE

Before you begin creating your vision, I'd like to warn you to be careful for what you wish for. I've worked with so many clients who have accumulated great wealth and succeeded financially, but something is still missing – peace, love, connection or happiness. You'd think having plenty of money and options would bring everything, right? It seems not. After digging deeper, it's clear that some people listen to their heads far more then their hearts and their values. It's like working hard to achieve a goal, perhaps buying a new car or getting a promotion, only to find that the feeling of success is short-lived. When we go after external success and ignore what we really need, what we really value, we might forget to align with what the heart deeply desires!

I think the key to a happy and content life is to follow your heart in everything you do, especially when it comes to creating a vision. The rest will come and you'll be on the right path for authentic success!. Whatever you want to bring towards you, listen to your heart first: is it something you really want to be doing, is it something that makes your heart sing? If so, then use your imagination to create it, feel it in your heart as you take action and peruse your passion. Follow your head rather than your heart and you may find you get the money, buy the car, meet the perfect partner, but still not have a solid foundation and still feel empty. Then you might end up chasing even more illusions and feeling even more unhappy, because you got what your ego wanted rather than what your soul needed.

The best outcomes happen when you follow your heart!

⊕ **Transforming your destiny**

Close your eyes and think about what you've learnt so far in this chapter, what your heart wants, where you want to go and the vision your wrote down earlier. Where do you see yourself in the future? Spend a few minutes relaxing and breathing in and out. Pay attention to your breath and let your body relax. You can scan your body and connect to your inner world as we did in the previous meditations (see Chapter 1, page 24-8 and 51-2). As you focus on your breath go deeper and relax.

Now imagine taking a quantum leap into your future. Create your success in your mind's eye and leap five or ten years into the future. Imagine how your life looks and feels now you've achieved everything you set out to achieve in your vision.

* How does your future self look?

* How do you speak, think and feel?

* Where are you and what are you doing?

* Who are you with, and what are people saying to you now you have succeeded?

You might see yourself in a number of pictures, looking healthy, happy or wealthy, or you mind might just focus on one picture. Whatever you tune into, bring your vision closer to your mind's eye and play it out like you're watching a movie on the big screen.

Now make the colours brighter and tune into any sensations you feel. You may feel excited, proud or confident, because you nailed it and created the life you really wanted. You might feel safe, free and loved, because you've found that special someone. Whatever feelings and images you tune into, turn up the colours and the volume to the max!

Make it bigger and expand your vision so you're watching it in HD and then use your imagination to step into your movie. Start walking towards your future self. Look into his or her eyes and in your mind say hello. Make a connection to your future self. Keep breathing. Relax. Let your imagination paint your new world as you connect to your future self.

Your future self might have a message for you. He or she might have something to tell you, ask them questions if you feel the need to, or ask them what you need to do to create the epic life they're living. Pay attention, listen carefully to the answers you receive and let your mind do all the work. Imagine you're having a chat with your best friend and they have the answers.

When you're ready, ask them to show you what your new life is like. Visualize the places, people and things in your life. Maybe you live somewhere else, have new friends, travel to new places, have a better relationship with your family, have more money, better health, higher energy, or feel happy, clean and free, or you're following your passion and getting paid to live your purpose.

If your vision is to lose weight, see yourself in perfect health, working out and eating a healthy diet. If you want to create success and wealth, see your new business, or check your bank account and see some extra zeros in there. If your dream is to write a book, see yourself at your book launch signing copies or typing away on your computer. Whatever you want to create, see yourself in the future enjoying your new world, taking action and embracing your authentic success!

Now for the best bit!

Imagine your future self stepping into your body so you become one person. As they step into you, feel every atom within your body reconnect with the reality that this is your future: this is your world. Now walk around in your new world and, this time, see the vision through your own eyes, rather than looking from the outside or watching your future self lap it up. Now you are walking around in this world and you can feel the success within every cell of your body, turn the feelings up, expand the vision, feel the emotions, make it bigger and brighter and really take a journey into your vision by using your imagination. Notice as much detail about your vision as possible. Maybe the sky seems brighter; you can smell the flowers or feel the breeze on your body. Whatever you feel and see, paint this picture in your mind's eye and let your imagination run wild! You should feel excited and alive as you tune into your vision and what you see and feel should light you up, make you feel excited and ready for action! Make sure you paint a vivid picture before moving on to the next stage.

When you're ready, and you feel like you want to explode with joy, make the picture bigger and brighter one last time. Remind yourself how amazing you are and how this vision feels and then take a visual snapshot of it, then send that picture right through the centre of your forehead. Imagine downloading your vision from your future and sending it through your head and into your brain. Imagine your vision travelling through your forehead and connecting to the centre of your brain, connecting to all the neurons and electricity inside your head. Let your mind hardwire your vision into your brain and create new programs and patterns that this is your new reality. Tell your mind this picture is your new destiny and install a subconscious belief by repeating the mantra, 'This is my new reality, this is my new reality, this is my new reality.' You can use other mantras such as, 'I can,' 'I am' or 'I will' or make your own up. Reinforce to your mind that you are going to smash it and make it happen!

Now blast your vision down from your brain and into your body, down your spine, your nervous system and all around you. Let it connect and ignite within every single cell in your body. Feel your vision move up and down your entire body, from the top of your head to the tips of your toes. FEEL IT!

For a moment just sit with the feelings and sensations in your body. Let your vision do its magic! When you are ready, send everything you have just felt and visualized into your heart. Keep it in your heart and feel the love, peace and joy deep inside. If you like, you can also blast that picture from your heart back out into the universe. Blast the image towards your future, send the love to your family and friends or keep it in your heart and embrace it.

When you are ready, slowly and gently open your eyes.

Feel free to adapt this technique, play around with it and make it your own but, for the best results, allocate some time to do this every day for at least 30 days. I usually visualize as soon as I wake up in the morning and before I get out of bed. I stick my headphones on, close my eyes and use my imagination to dream big. And it has never let me down!

To help you stay on track, I've created a step-by-step guided visualisation download in your membership area (www.wakethefckup.com), so you can start rewiring your brain for success. You might also like to use the following tried-and-tested techniques to help keep you walking on the path of a visionary in the coming days, months, years.

....

SIX OF THE BEST VISIONARY TOOLS

Learning and gaining more knowledge is one of the biggest keys to personal success and below are six of the best ideas I've come across to help turn visions into reality.

#1 CREATE A VISION BOARD

A vision board is just a fancy title for a collection of images and words that inspire you. You can choose to create one on your computer desktop, on a site like Pinterest or on a large piece of card. The key thing is to position your vision board where you'll see it most often so that it reminds you where you are heading.

So go grab some magazines or head to your computer and start selecting any words or images that inspire you. It might be pictures of countries you want to visit, people you want to meet, healthy food, people who are into fitness, a motorbike, a new home, or a car. Remember to focus on what your heart wants and have fun with it.

Every day take a few minutes to look at your vision board and absorb the images into your mind. Look at it, breathe deeply, close your eyes and enter your vision.

#2 CREATE A MIND MOVIE

A mind movie is basically a vision board that plays as a movie. Search the Internet and download any pictures that align with your vision, then create your own personal slide show or use some fancy software like Final Cut Pro to create a mini movie. You might also want to add a soundtrack. Choose some music that really gets you going, makes you feel motivated and inspired. Every day, preferably before you do anything else, take some time to watch your movie – just breathe deeply and tune into the sounds and images you're hearing and seeing. As you watch your movie, feel your vibration rising and let that positive, upbeat energy about where you're headed start your day.

#3 WRITE A $10 MILLION CHEQUE

When comedian and actor Jim Carrey was broke and struggling as an actor, he wrote himself out a cheque for $10 million as an affirmation of what he would be earning one day. Every now and then he would go for a drive, park up, take out his cheque and visualize his success. He would picture what his future looked like as he activated the Law of Attraction and just doing that made him feel wealthy. A few years later, he was cast in the movie *Dumb and Dumber* and, boom, the rest is history!

You might not be interested in making millions, but having tangible cues for your vision keeps reminding your subconscious mind what you want and how to get it. For two years I had a picture of Jack Canfield's book *The Success Principles* stuck to my ceiling. Every morning when I woke up, I visualized the day I'd meet him and thank him for his message in *The Secret*. This year I did meet him and he pulled me on stage. After his workshop he sat next to me and looked me straight in the eye, we shook hands and I was able to give him my letter of thanks. If you are looking for extra cash, what cheque would you write and how much for?

#4 DECLARE YOUR DREAMS

Part of dreaming big is declaring your vision to others, so tell your friends and family, blog it, post it on Facebook or tweet out to the world. You've got to be bold and declare and share your vision with other people, because it sends the message to your mind, and out into the universe, that you're serious about your mission. Going public will mean that some people will laugh at you, but you'll also find that if you share your vision with your true friends and family they will support you and keep you accountable. Some might even tell you that you're dreaming too small and to aim higher. Taking big leaps of faith and sharing your vision encourages others to dream big and act bolder too. It's almost like you give them permission to go after the vision they've secretly been dreaming of too!

#5 TAKE AN ATTITUDE OF GRATITUDE

Another epic strategy is to thank the universe for what you want to attract. Write down, 'Thank you universe for . . .' and then fill in the blanks. Here's an example of some of the things that have been on my list recently, many of which have come true.

* Thank you, universe, for my health and happiness.
* Thank you, universe, for my trip to Thailand.
* Thank you, universe, for my book deal.
* Thank you, universe, for my £10 million.

Think about what you want; then thank the universe for already having it. Act as if you already have it and really cultivate a sense of appreciation and gratitude.

#6 STAY COMMITTED

I think the reason most people give up on their dreams is because they don't see immediate results. They put in a little work, dream up a better life in their mind, wish for a better life and expect change to happen over night. But then they hit the first roadblock and give up, or keep dreaming about a better life but don't take action. As you can probably guess, I love using the power of my imagination to create the life I love living, but nothing meaningful has ever fallen out of the sky without me putting in the work. I see it as a two-way process, I think the vision and hand it over to the universe then I get off my arse and take massive action to make it happen. You have to vow to yourself you will never give up or quit when the going gets tough. You have to stay committed to your dreams no matter how far away you think they are or how many people laugh at you!

Most of us dream too small!

Remember, it takes the same amount of energy to dream small and attract what you don't want, as it does to dream HUGE and attract what you do want. As a final note on vision, try not get so carried away thinking about tomorrow that you forget to live your life for today and connect to the beauty of now. As Jack Canfield says, it's about having '110 per cent expectation and zero attachment' to your goals. So, as you fly towards your future, remember this is your life and it's happening right NOW. Set aside some time for strategizing about what you really want to get out of life and then get out there, connect, make it happen and enjoy the ride!

Chapter 4

ENGINEERING YOUR CHANGE

'THE ONLY WAY TO MAKE SENSE OUT OF CHANGE IS TO PLUNGE INTO IT, MOVE WITH IT, AND JOIN THE DANCE.' Alan Watts

19 APRIL 2005

'Look, I know I've f#cked up again. I can't help myself. This is killing me!'

The musky smell of incense lingered in the air. Buddhist monks walked around holding their bowls while tourists snapped away and rubbed gold leaf over the Buddha statues. I was out of prison but this time down on my knees praying for help in a little temple in Pattaya, Thailand.

'I'll do anything, just show me a way out! I know I've not committed myself to changing. I know I'm getting worse, but I don't know what to do any more. I need some guidance.'

After another psychotic night on the drugs, I was desperate for a way out but a temple was the last place on Earth I thought I'd end up, especially in Pattaya! The place was a sex heaven. Booze, sex and drugs on tap 24/7 – and I was addicted to the lot! But, just like in Carshalton, the fun had disappeared and I felt lost in Thailand.

It had been a few years since I'd had my epiphany in my cell reading *Moment by Moment*, but I was worse than ever before. I'd done another prison sentence in between, and the vision for a better life was slowly slipping away. Pattaya had become a living nightmare. I was losing the will to live! The night before, I'd locked myself in a room with a Thai girl I'd met in a go-go bar. We drank bottles of Chang beer and downed cheap whisky. Smoked yabba (Thailand's crazy drug), snorted coke and did ecstasy!

As usual; I got paranoid and withdrew into my darker suicidal thoughts and the voices that told me to end it all.

At one point, in the middle of the night, I was sweating and delirious, looking over the edge of the balcony thinking about jumping to the ground to finish it all. I just wanted to escape the psychosis – the demons in my mind seemed so real and were driving me insane!

Thankfully Dad's Thai wife took me to the temple the next day. Somehow, just like that moment in the prison library, I felt a real sense of peace amid the chaos. As I found myself praying, I felt the hairs on my arms rise and every cell in my body merged with something spiritual. I felt connected to something bigger and spookier than me, it felt powerful but calm and so I prayed and begged for more direction.

'Just give me the strength to change, just give me a little nudge to get me on the right path. I'll put the work in, I promise.'

I didn't believe in God, or half the Buddhist stories about reincarnation, but I knew something was looking out for me, I believed in karma and technically I should have been dead. So I bowed my head and silently made another vow to get back on the right path. I sent Ella and my mum more love and apologized for not being there for them. Even though I felt like I was a million miles away from home, being in the little temple, in the presence of the monks, I felt at home.

When I walked out of the temple, I promised myself that this time it would be different. I was committed 110 per cent. It was do or die. I knew what I had to do. The inner voice was getting louder and doing its best to steer me in the right direction. I just had to pay attention and take action.

When I arrived back in the UK, I crashed on Dad's sofa for a couple of nights. I was wrecked from all the booze and yabba and took a few days to detox. **Dad left me to sweat it out, but I knew I couldn't outstay my welcome. He always gave the tough-love approach, but I also knew he wanted me out of his flat so he could rebuild *his* life and get off drugs too. When I finally woke up, I packed my belongings into two black bin bags and left Carshalton for good.**

CHANGE: COURAGEOUS STEPS TOWARDS WAKING THE F#CK UP!

It takes a lot of courage and strength to wake up and make big changes in your life, so I'm not going to airbrush it and make out that transformation is easy. If it was, everyone would be doing it! Change takes time, and the road to personal success can be tricky. But in the same way that an acorn grows into a f#ck-off big oak tree, we are wired to grow and stretch ourselves. It's in our biology! When we choose to change and grow, we go beyond the limitations in our ego and what others think. We even surprise ourselves! By learning new skills and stretching ourselves, we gain more confidence and self-belief and conquer our fears. In the end, those goals and dreams that seemed a million miles away become our new lifestyle.

Taking a leap of faith can be scary. For many of us, change seems too daunting so we avoid it like the plague. We stick to what we know best, even if it frustrates the sh#t out of us. We know we have certain areas in our lives that need to change, patterns that need to be broken because they are holding us back from our goals and dreams, but most of us avoid them and keep on going.

Some changes are small, perhaps giving up certain foods, spending more time in the gym, controlling our spending habits, giving up weed, or cutting down on the cheeky bottle of wine every night. However, other changes can feel gigantic, like moving away, starting life again, getting off hard drugs, ending a relationship, starting a business, or handing in your notice to follow your passion and purpose. Change can feel terrifying for some of us, and exciting for others. It's the way we choose to look at change that makes all the difference. I have found that change equals growth, and it's key to waking up and succeeding in life.

No matter how big or small the change seems to you right now, it's your opportunity to take control and succeed. The bigger the change, the bigger the success! The process of change is the same for all of us. We have to be brave, act bold and fearless even if we feel unsure, anxious or worried. Fake it until you make it, act with courage and confidence, and you'll notice that each step you take, and every challenge along the way makes you stronger and more determined to succeed. Before you know it, you've changed an area in your life that once seemed too big to change.

Now you've created a new vision, you might start to notice that you need to bring change to certain areas of your life. Once we've decided we want something new, it highlights what's holding us back. Don't be put off or by looking at the size of the mountain, let it inspire you and know that if you take the first step you'll reach the top quicker than you think.

You have two choices: avoid change and let your vision slip away from you, or take charge and smash it!

When I left Carshalton I didn't have a clue what I was doing or where I'd end up. I never thought I'd be sitting by the beach typing these words or appearing in a film with Richard Branson. No one jumps from A to Z overnight! The first step is always the hardest, but it's usually the most rewarding because it gives you the confidence to keep going. When I look back now, it was obvious I'd succeed because I followed a process and took the first step. When we dig deep, face our fears and take that leap, we grow into our vision.

STAYING STUCK!

I'm sure you know people who don't change; some are afraid, some are stuck in their old ways and patterns, while others choose to be right all the time and simply choose not to grow. They stay stuck for years, same problems, same issues, same dramas – same sh#t, different day! It turns out life is an upward spiral and if we want to experience more of the good stuff then we need to move with nature just as it was intended. What I mean by this is that everything in nature is growing and evolving: our pets age, trees get taller, flowers blossom and we get older. Even weeds grow through concrete just to reach the sun! Human beings are part of that natural world and it's in our blueprint to grow. That's why those who are always learning more, stretching themselves and growing are usually a lot happier, more successful and fulfilled than those who stay stuck, stagnant and stressed but don't take action and come up with a million reasons why they can't.

Stop making excuses!

There's no point making excuses for not changing. Believe me, I've heard them all. People even pay me thousands of pounds for my coaching packages and still make excuses. They're too busy, scared of failure or moan and end up being too lazy to get cracking! Making excuses kills your dreams, robs you of energy and keeps you stuck on the same path. Here's a few of the excuses I hear over and over again:

* I'd love to do yoga, but I'm too stiff and unfit.
* I'd love to eat healthily, but it's hard to find the time.
* I'd love to start a business, but I'm broke.
* I'd love to travel, but I don't have anyone to go with.
* I'd love to follow my passion, but I don't have the energy.
* I'd love to follow my purpose, but I'm not sure what it is yet.
* I'd love to meditate, but my thoughts are too busy and I can't sit still.
* I'd love to have time off with my kids, but I'm too busy.

Can you see the paradox in these lame excuses? When you get off your arse and actually do it, instead of talking about it and procrastinating, you eliminate the original problem. What's more, unless you get up and take action the excuse will always stop you from succeeding. The more I moaned and bitched about writing this book over the years, the less productive time I actually spent writing it.

⊕ **Get real**

Get real with yourself: spot the excuses you are making about change and write them down in your journal now.

PERSONAL CHANGE

Since the day you arrived on this amazing planet, you've been moving through the process of change and personal success. So why stop now? From day one, you've been learning: how to crawl, walk, talk, run. Joined sports teams, asked your first crush out on a date, plucked up the courage to pucker up for your first kiss (and the rest of it), left school and got your first job, and I'm sure there have been a number of areas in your life that you've changed and adapted. Sometimes we choose to change, sometimes change smacks us in the face, like the birth of a child or the loss of a family member or friend. Either way, we usually find the strength to carry on and move through the adjustments life throws at us.

....

CRAZY CHANGE AHEAD

Just over a decade or two ago, the idea of photos from the surface of Mars and tourists taking trips out into orbit would have been unimaginable except in sci-fi movies. Or how about talking to someone on the other side of the world on a handheld device? Closer to home, social networking barely existed 15 years ago, but it's now part of our reality and many of us would struggle to live without it! We live in a world that thrives on social change as history continually shifts and is reshaping itself.

We are changing the way we live and producing more information every year than in all the previous years put together, so why does it seem so difficult to change our lives. Why do we feel so uncomfortable with such a natural process? Why are so many people stuck in a rut or still playing the cards they were dealt when they don't need? This is all down to the illusion of fear and an ego that tells you change is something to avoid, that it's going to be too hard, too painful, too dangerous.

....

Think about it, all the changes you've made in your life up until now have got you to where you are. Admittedly, you might be reading this book because you want more from life, you want to break away from the crowd and you're not where you want to be yet. However, everything you have been through, all the changes, choices and decisions you've made in some way shape or form, have served your purpose and here you are now! I know it may seem like there is a huge gap between where you are now and where you want to be, but you only need to see the first step and get moving in the right direction to reap the rewards later in life. The decisions you make today are the birth of your future!

....

◉ Thinking about change

If you feel stuck in any area of your life right now, or you really want to adapt a certain area of your life, think about the thoughts you think and the feelings you feel when you think about changing, growing, succeeding or giving something up. Write them down in your journal and be honest with yourself. It's normal to fear change or feel negative towards it when your ego is running the show. By the end of this chapter your mindset will have shifted and you'll view change as something epic and be racing headlong towards it.

....

GETTING COMFY WITH DISCOMFORT

The trouble is, doing what you've always done or following the same old patterns since childhood is learnt behaviour. It feels comfortable and you know what results you'll get. But in the long run, it can also keep us stuck in unwanted patterns and might stop us from growing and succeeding in life. In the end it's the comfort zone that becomes uncomfortable because deep down we know we want more from life but we talk ourselves out of it, or should I say the ego talks you out of it!

For the past 10 years I've lived outside my comfort zone, I've been facing my fears, stepping it up, getting it wrong and making a ton of mistakes along the way. After a few years I realized that's where true success happens. Outside the comfort zone! We won't achieve our dreams living inside the boxes and playing it safe. Your personal success is out there in the unknown territory that makes you feel uneasy.

The great yogis tell us to get comfortable in our discomfort, which is why some yoga postures look insane! If you want to create something new in your life and are determined to achieve your vision, then fear will inevitably arise and you'll feel funny about it. You might try to avoid that inner feeling or even doubt yourself. The first thing that we need to understand is that feeling uncomfortable about change is a natural part of the process. It serves as a sign to let you know you are on the right path and that something new and amazing is just around the corner.

This discomfort might pop up in the form of negative thoughts, such as 'I'm not good enough, who am I kidding?', or you might feel it in the pit of your stomach – a heavy, anxious fear will arise and make you feel sick when you think about making certain changes in your life. Most people will throw in the towel before they even begin. They'll think about the changes they want to make in their lives, then feel the uncomfortable feelings arise and their negative thoughts will talk them out of it.

Whatever challenges you face, however you feel and whatever your monkey mind tries to tell you about avoiding change, greet your discomfort as a positive experience and mindfully breathe through the emotions and observe the thoughts. Remember, you are the hotel, and your thoughts and feelings are only guests.

The more you face the things you fear, the faster your fear will disappear.

◎ Identifying change

To help you uncover the big or small changes you wish to make in your life, start by thinking about what needs to change and what you want to achieve. Then recognize how the idea of the change makes you feel. Just note what comes up for you and sit with those feelings for a while. Note down your answers to the following questions in your journal.

* What areas of your life feel uncomfortable?
* What keeps you awake at night with stress or worry?
* What needs to change in your life?
* What do you want to overcome, give up or let go of?
* What behaviours/habits do you keep repeating?
* What do you really want to achieve but feel afraid of when you think about it?

* What do you really want from life but talk yourself out of?
* Who do you really want to become but talk yourself out of becoming?

....

Many of the people I've worked with over the years admit to wasting a lot of time and energy moaning about their current situation, getting frustrated and annoyed with themselves and procrastinating rather than taking action to move closer towards a life that excites them. Change begins by accepting responsibility for your choices and the future improvements you wish to make and then taking the first step.

Of course, no one likes ending a relationship, quitting a job, running on the treadmill for 30 minutes when it's sunny outside, packing their bags and leaping, or saying 'No thanks, no more cookies or crack for me, I'm eating carrots and getting clean today!' But take the first step, even if you're afraid, and the rest will be history. Before you know it, you'll be looking back and be blown away at how far you've come and how much you've achieved. The small changes are fundamental if you want to take big leaps in your life.

Meet Pete

Giving up any drug can often seem impossible. Especially when you've been using it for more than half your life. Pete was in his fifties and had been using heroin for 30 years, injecting in his groin and taking methadone. But no matter what state he was in, he always spoke to me like I was a mate. On this day I remember being in the drop-in centre and showing everyone my photos from a recent trip to Thailand. Pete took a look and all of a sudden his face changed, he went white and looked as though he'd seen a ghost. His eyes welled up and he held the emotions back as he blurted out, 'That's Grieg!'

Grieg was a monk from Thamkrabok. Many years ago he was a heroin addict and flew out to Thailand to get recovery. He liked it there so much that he never left and was ordained as a monk for life. On my recent visit he'd taken me under his wing and showed me around the temple.

'Brett, I used to be Grieg's best mate. We both lived in Guildford and used together. I thought he was dead.' Part of me was gobsmacked and had the usual thoughts about it being a small world, while another part of me knew that everything happens for a reason.

In a split second Pete made a decision to change and decided he was going to Thailand to get clean and see Grieg. Over the next month we raised enough money to buy Pete a return ticket to Thailand and get him to the detox. Pete did a sponsored walk and walked 11 miles a day and people donated what they could. For a smack head that was pretty good going! Pete acted on inspiration and charged towards his vision. Within months Pete flew out to Thailand and met Grieg and got clean. Sadly, Grieg passed away just after Pete met him. I guess it was meant to be. A year after Pete got clean, I flew out to Thailand and was best man at his wedding.

No one knows where change will take them, but the successful ones start at the beginning and work their way up.

FOCUS, FOCUS, FOCUS!

One of the biggest mistakes we can make is worrying, moaning and stressing about all the stuff we can't change. Bitching about things you can't control usually means never taking action to change the things you can. When I learnt how to brain dump and let go of the stuff I couldn't control and just focus on the things I could change, I felt so much lighter and was able to create changes a lot quicker. In the next exercise, you'll unpack everything you have in your baggage and find out how to let go of the stuff you can't control.

⊙ Taking control of change

List all the things you worry about. You know the sh#t you obsess about, find yourself thinking about in the middle of the night, complain about, moan to your mates about. For instance, your list might include:

* Paying the gas bill at the end of the month
* The price of petrol
* Your spouse/partner's drinking
* The weather
* The size of your nose (or any other part of your body)
* Your weight
* Your addictions
* Your lack of money

Take this opportunity to have a proper brain dump and make a list of all the crap that swirls around in your mind, the stuff you stress and grumble about.

Now take a look at your list and put a circle around all the things you can control. For example, someone who wrote the above list would circle,

* Paying the gas bill at the end of the month

* Your weight

* Your addictions

* Your lack of money

Write the controllable items on a new page and we'll come back to them in a minute.

Now look at your original list and all the stuff you worry about but have no control over. No matter how powerful or positive you are, you can't control the weather, someone else's drinking habit, the size of your nose (unless you have cosmetic surgery, but that's another story) or the price of petrol. Giving attention to this stuff is just a waste of your time and energy which would be better spent taking action to control the things you can change.

Whatever worries you wrote down, it's time to let go of them. Close your eyes and tell your mind to let each one go in turn. Have a silent chat with yourself about what's important to you and how you plan to focus your time and energy in future. Then open your eyes and cross each worry off the list and, silently or aloud, tell yourself, 'I'm choosing to let go of this sh#t right now!'

Now go back to the second list you wrote out. I'm sure you can guess where this is going! This is the list of worries that you have total control over. Concentrate your efforts on it because changing those things will radically change your life for the better! So let's hatch a simple plan.

For each worry you have on your list, write down one action that you could take in the next 24 hours to deal with it. For instance, you could buy a yoga mat on Amazon instead of watching TV at night to help you get fit, or go through your budget to see where you're overspending, or pick up the phone and book yourself a coaching session with a drug and alcohol counsellor. I can still remember the day I booked my first counselling session. I was nervous, felt silly, weak and thought it was going to be a load of rubbish. It turns out it was the best thing I ever did! If I'd listened to my ego and worried about the pointless sh#t, and let my fears and other people's comments take over, then chances are I would never have sorted my sh#t out and I wouldn't be here now!

··

THE ILLUSION OF FEAR

As I described in Chapter 1, the ego doesn't want to be your enemy, it's just trying to keep you safe and out of harm's way. For example, the other day I was in a Tube station in my own little world when I tripped up the steps and my hands automatically reached out in front of me. I didn't think about it, it was a reflex reaction. Even if your hands are in your pockets they'll get out as quick as they can to try to stop your fall so you don't hurt yourself. They protect you automatically. Just like a cat always lands on its feet, I guess!

Your mind and body have this incredible inner mechanism to keep you safe and they are always trying to protect you from danger. What's more, when you experience pain throughout your life, then your inner protector works its magic and stores a pain and danger memory inside your brain. Next time you see steps you might remember how you fell, so you'll go a little slower and be more mindful.

The problem is, sometimes pain simply represents the *possibility* of danger and makes us subconsciously fearful that we might fall flat on our face. So we don't leave a dead-end job because we fear we'll never find another one. We stay in environments that cause us more harm than good and go along with the crowd, because we fear that we'll never make new friends and end up like Billy no mates. Or we give up on our goals in case we fail, look stupid and it doesn't work out. We don't deliberately set out to play it safe and most people aren't aware of this inner mechanism because it happens at a deeper, subconscious, biological level. But chances are you will notice some inner conflict within you because you might desperately want something new and different in your life, or dream about your goals, but underneath you feel fearful of taking action, you stay in your comfort zone and your inner protector keeps you safe. Your ego will do everything and anything within its power to talk you out of change and keep you safe. It hates being wrong, losing control, so you have to face it head on!

Fear does not always give us a good representation of danger – quite often it's just an illusion!

⊕ **Challenge yourself**

Think of something that will take you out of your comfort zone
and challenge you to face your fear and sit with your discomfort.
It might be something silly like speaking to everyone in
Japanese for the day (well, blag it, and pretend you're talking
Japanese unless you know how to!), or asking 10 random people
for their phone number or walking into KFC and ordering
a Chinese! Do something that makes you feel embarrassed,
awkward and uncomfortable. Choose to experience the
uncomfortable feelings inside you instead of always avoiding
them.

FACE YOUR FEARS AND SEE WHAT HAPPENS

It's funny, I've always been great at talking to people but when I
first started public speaking and running workshops my body was
terrified. My legs shook like Elvis Presley's, my mouth dried up like
Gandhi's flip-flops and I had this horrible feeling in the pit of my
stomach. I've spent years learning the art of public speaking and
doing crazy techniques to help me overcome the fear. A few years
ago I did walk into KFC and order a Chinese. As I waited in the queue,
knowing that I felt nervous because my ego was about to be exposed
and I was going to look pretty silly, I felt anxious and wanted to run
away. My mind darted all over the place as I thought about how others
would react to my random request and I knew the lady behind the
counter would think I was bonkers!

When you choose to embarrass your ego and look silly, your
body will probably react, you'll feel this anxiety and worry sweep

through you. The fight or flight response will kicks in and you'll want to leg it. If not, then you're not stretching yourself enough, so think of something that will take you outside your comfort zone and do it this week. I challenge you! Rather than staying safe in familiar feelings or avoiding them, you are choosing to experience discomfort and over time whatever you fear will disappear, even if it's the fear of public speaking or ordering a Chinese in KFC!

FOCUS ON YOUR WHY

Once we face our fears head on and begin to get comfy with discomfort, ask yourself why you really want to change in the first place. Understanding your why is vital in staying committed to change and is one of the keys to personal success, because it will remind you why you are making big changes in your life when things get tough or you want to give up. Digging deep for your why exposes the real pain, rather than the illusion of fear and danger. And your real pain will motivate you into action! For example, you may be in debt, broke and struggling to pay your bills when you decide enough is enough and sort your finances out or finally you start your own business. When the going gets tough and you feel like giving up, you can remind yourself how painful it was being broke, how much you stressed and worried about money and how you used to dream about having more time off with the family and treating your children. You might decide you want to start a campaign against animal cruelty, but not have the first idea where to begin, or how to set up a website or whether anyone will join in your quest. When you take the time out to think about how the animals are treated, killed and slaughtered and connect to the pain you feel, your why will inspire you into action. Or perhaps being overweight is really getting you down and every time you look in the mirror you feel upset – this will be your why for going to the gym, cutting out fizzy drink and switching to juicing!

When you remind yourself of the real pain and why you are changing, your passion kicks in and motivates you to succeed even more. This may sound obvious, but most people don't focus on their why and life is 'comfortable' or they feel stuck and frustrated. If they do decide to change, they often hit the first challenge and quit after a few weeks because they forget the pain and don't remind themselves why they decided to change in the first place. When you focus on your why, it takes over your life and pushes you forward.

··

◉ Finding your why

Now you have a vision and are choosing to move in a new direction, it's important to understand why you want to move forward. Write down all the areas of your life that you want to change or have been thinking about changing, or have been avoiding for some time. Chances are they are blocking you from achieving your vision and over time this will drain your energy and work against you. Once you've written out your list, write down against each area or behaviour why you want to change it. Why does it mean so much to you to change this area of your life, how will your life be different once you change it or overcome it, and who will you be once you've done so? Or how will your life look in 10 years from now if you don't change that area or behaviour?

··

If you want to stay committed to change, know your why.

If you choose to take one small step in an area of your life now, then in 10, 20, 30 years your life will have better outcomes. On the other hand, if you choose not to change, the consequences could be dramatic. Leaving Carshalton meant leaving everything I knew – my friends, my family and even my daughter, Ella – but I know staying would have killed me. I would have been doing more prison sentences, the drugs would have got harder and some silly bugger would have caught up with me in the pub and it would have kicked off big time. My why was so big, you could say it was life or death, so I took a huge leap forwards and since then I've never looked back. Every time I make a change now, I connect to the real pain of not changing and it kicks me into gear.

SIX SHIFTS FOR POSITIVE CHANGE

Sometimes you've got to fake it until you make it and talk yourself into taking action, even if you're afraid and feeling doubtful. But ultimately you want to create a winning mindset so you can view change in a new light, feel excited about the adventure ahead and ignite enough passion to take action. Before you begin making change, always ask yourself these three questions:

* Do I want to accomplish something?
* Do I want to experience something?
* Do I want to be someone?

Below are six powerful mind shifts for making positive changes in your life. They have transformed my attitude towards making change and you may find them helpful when you think about the life you are destined to create too!

#1 GET CLEAR

The first step to getting what you want out of life and making big changes is to get crystal clear about what you want to achieve. Write down three goals in each of the following seven areas:

Financial goals

Business and career goals

Family time and connection goals

Health and wellness goals

Relationship goals

Personal growth goals

Making a difference goals

Be as specific as you can when focusing on these areas and find your why. Write down your goals in as much detail as possible and review them daily. Preferably in the morning before you do anything else! One of the main reasons why people don't get what they want out of life and find it hard to get rid of unwanted habits is that they are not clear about what it is they really want. When you've set your goals, picture your success inside your mind – remember, the power of your imagination is where your success lies!

#2 FOCUS ON THE END RESULTS

Short-term pain puts people off and so they never change. They procrastinate because of the discomfort, worry about the burn, feel anxious about the side effects or don't want to face the effort it takes to change, so they never get started. But like discomfort, the short-term pain is the positive feedback you need to receive; it lets you know that you're on the right path. When you feel the burn that's the time to dig deeper and keep going. Focus on your long-term results, close your eyes and envision your success. Think about where you'll be in 10 years' time if you keep going.

Some people give up just as they are about to have a major breakthrough because they take their eyes off the prize and get consumed by the short-term pain. Silently ask yourself, 'If I keep going, where will this lead me in the end?'

#3 STAY COMMITTED

Everyone has days when they want to quit, fall off the wagon, eat a greasy takeaway, splurge on a credit card or run upstairs and hide under the covers. Make a commitment to bring your vision into reality and take a silent vow to yourself that this is your chosen path and no matter how hard it gets, or how many times you slip up, you'll keep going, dust yourself off and always start again!

Accept that challenges will arise, people will doubt you, you'll doubt yourself, you'll feel tired, bored or confused, you'll relapse, screw up, feel overwhelmed and wonder if it's all worth it. This is normal! This is the process of change at work. What makes all the difference is how committed you stay and whether you keep going. Each time you fall, know that falling is part of your success. You are on the right road, keep going!

#4 SUCCESS IS INEVITABLE

When you go on holiday you follow a simple process. You check your passport's in date, pick a destination, book a hotel and your flights, get some money exchanged and buy some new shades. Before you know it you're kicking back on the beach with the sun beating down on you and your toes in the sand as you listen to the waves.

If you didn't follow the process, or you missed out a step such as booking your flights, then chances are you won't be going anywhere. The same holds true for creating your epic adventure. If you work out the steps that you need to take and then take action, you'll achieve what you want to achieve. You just need to follow the process. Waking up isn't rocket science. Drill it into your mind that success is inevitable if you keep going!

Think about some of the goals you wrote down earlier and chunk them down into smaller actions. What are the steps: first, second, third, fourth and fifth? Chunk them down into five steps and the change won't feel so intimidating and you'll be flying to your destination before you know it!

#5 NO FAILURE, ONLY FEEDBACK

There are no mistakes in life if we learn from them and do something differently the next time. If we repeat the same challenges in life then we're not learning and will never get the results we really want. Challenges and setbacks are there to remind you where you're headed and reveal more about yourself. So welcome your mistakes, even the ones you feel gutted about making, investigate them a little deeper, because you know that when you're making 'mistakes' you're moving closer to your vision. If I'd known this mindset shift years ago I would have been so much kinder to myself when I screwed up. I used to hate on myself real bad and it kept me in the vicious cycle.

This is also called learning from your mistakes and that's an important distinction, because most of us beat ourselves when we f#ck up! Instead of turning against yourself, tune out the criticism and connect to your louder voice and start looking at what you can learn from the mistake, be kind to yourself and then set off again. In this way you fail your way forwards. This mindset shift is incredibly empowering, because it means you are never making mistakes, just growing and learning how to get it right for next time. I love it!

Think back to the last time you feel like you messed up. Investigate your screw-ups and ask yourself, 'What did I learn from that?' When you reflect on past challenges, you'll probably notice you learn a lot more than you expected to. There are no f#ck ups, only feedback.

#6 STRETCH YOURSELF

When leaping forwards and taking control of your life, it's important to set goals and dreams that stretch you – it's the only way to grow. Going beyond your limitations, setting big goals and stretching yourself beyond what you thought was possible is the key to your personal success. You want to be making quantum leaps into your future so big that they fire you up and frighten you at the same time. This way your consciousness expands and works out the route for you. For instance ,a big stretch could be writing a book, starting a business, losing 20 pounds, making your first million, buying a home by the sea, building a school in Africa, getting married or never drinking again.

Remember, material goals are symbols of our inner success. When we grow inside we create and attract more on the outside. The great thing about stretching yourself internally is that the benefits will last forever. You could lose all the material stuff overnight – the book might be a flop, the house might burn down – but, unlike an elastic band, once you've stretched your mind and your consciousness it can never go back to its original form or old ways of thinking and being.

◉ Rewire your brain for change

Some people like to start each day with a mantra or let it be the last thing they think or say before going to sleep. Mantras can help rewire your thinking and make you feel powerful almost instantly. Here's one of my favourite mantras to help you head towards change feeling positive.

'I can. I am. I will.'

You say 'I can' because you know that humans have change wired into their DNA, so of course you can do it; 'I am' because you're already doing it; and 'I will' because you're choosing to change.

As you say the mantra, feel it in your core, pull your shoulders back and stand taller as you walk: 'I CAN. I AM. I WILL.'

Repeat this mantra whenever you face a challenge that seems bigger than you, whenever you feel nervous, or whenever you want more confidence and inner strength. Repeat it over and over and over or shout it out loud until those three phrases become the dominant thought pattern lodged inside your mind whenever you think about change.

Visit your online membership (www.wakethefckup.com) to download the MP3 to help you rewire your mindset for success. You can stick it on your smartphone or computer and listen to it every day, and it will guide you through some confidence-building mantras.

CHAPTER 5

ENGINEERING YOUR PATTERNS

'INSANITY: DOING THE SAME THING OVER AND OVER AGAIN AND EXPECTING DIFFERENT RESULTS.' Albert Einstein

8 DECEMBER 2007

'Just come out for one, it's your birthday.'

It was coming up to Christmas and I hadn't touched alcohol in months. Life was great! I felt happy and things were working out for me. I finally felt I'd got control of my life. I'd been living with Mum in Salisbury for two years and working as a drug and alcohol support worker for a big government-funded charity. I'd met new people in Salisbury, started going to the gym and had just bought myself a new car. The money was good, but more than that I loved my job. I was passionate and eager to make a difference to people's lives. I felt at home working with homeless people and addicts. I guess you could say I'd found my calling! Moving away from Carshalton was the best thing I ever did.

'OK, mate, I'll meet you down the bar,' I said, but something inside didn't feel right. In the shower, getting ready to go out, I felt odd – a sick, anxious feeling in my stomach, but I couldn't put my finger on it. I thought about staying in, watching a movie with Mum, but it was my birthday and I was doing well, so I made the decision to go out for one drink. As I dashed down the hill towards the club, I ignored the funny feeling in my gut and marched on.

The club was small but full when I got there. The house tunes were banging and I spotted a few fit chicks as I walked in. Before I knew it, I was at the bar knocking back shots of tequila. Even though I said I wouldn't get too wasted, one thing led to another and I ended up sinking pints of beer into the early hours. I was a lightweight without drugs and once I started drinking I couldn't stop. For me, drinking always ended the same way. I'd black out, get into some sort of trouble, kick off or forget what I did or where I was. This night was no different. I blacked out!

The next thing I knew I was behind the wheel of my new Astra driving 120mph up the M3. It was the middle of the night, there weren't many cars on the road, and it was like being on my own racetrack. I flew along the motorway like Nigel Mansell and pressed down harder on the accelerator, pushing the car to its limits. It was like I had a death wish and the alcohol and my ego were in charge. The speed sent a rush through my body. I felt this amazing high . . . right before I lost control.

The car spun out and smashed straight into the crash barrier. I whacked my head hard on the steering wheel and steam blew out from the engine. The warning lights on the dashboard flashed at me. Slipping in and out of consciousness, I tried to drive away but the car was f#cked! I blacked out again and woke up on the hard shoulder to blue lights flashing all around me. I could see the car was a wreck, but I was too drunk to acknowledge what I'd done or how serious it was. I blacked out for the final time and woke up the next morning in Woking police station.

As I peeled my head off the blue plastic mattress, I felt sick, the room was spinning and it took me a few minutes to work out why I was locked up. For a moment I drew a blank, I had no memory of the night before. Then, like a right hook from Muhammad Ali, the shame, worthlessness, and guilt suddenly hit me! *'What the f#ck have I done now?'* I asked myself as I dropped my head into my hands and burst into tears. '*F#ck! F#ck! F#ck!*'

I was gutted. I'd worked so hard to change my life. The more I thought about what I'd done, the more the memories flashed into my mind. '*Why didn't I just say no and stay in with Mum!*' I felt like I'd let myself down big time and reinforced my ego and its nasty thoughts that I was a failure. I'd blown everything. I'd moved away, cut down on my drinking and started my life over and now I'd f#cked it all up in one silly night. What was I going to say at work?

The copper came to the cell door and opened up. Perhaps he'd heard me crying, I'm not sure, but he looked sorry for me and told me I wasn't going to get bail and was due in court the next morning. I had a sickening feeling I was going back to prison. A familiar pattern I thought I'd escaped years ago! I had one phone call so I phoned work and told them only half the story.

PATTERNS: LIFE LESSONS WE REPEAT UNTIL WE WAKE THE F#CK UP AND BREAK THE CYCLE

Human beings are the smartest, most intelligent machines on the planet! We are amazing at recognizing patterns. We have the ability to identify them in their many forms, from getting dressed in the morning and going to work, to playing a game of chess and using apps on a smartphone, how the planets are spinning in the universe to understanding the rules of rugby! We also have the awareness to break unwanted patterns and create new empowering ones to really help us engineer the adventures we choose to take in life. One thing is clear, being able to recognize your personal patterns and breaking negative habits can create personal freedom and more success in your life.

By learning how to shape and improve our behaviours, we take a lot more control over our lives and where we're heading. Our pattern recognition is what gives us the edge over any other species in the animal kingdom. It's why mankind evolved to become rulers of the planet and it's how you're going to master your destiny! When it comes to transformation, recognizing and breaking any negative habitual patterns is key because it helps us get where we're headed faster.

So in this chapter we'll be exploring the conditioning, beliefs and unmet needs that are the source of all negative patterns, so you can create more awareness and then smash them!

SHAPED BY PATTERNS

Everything in this universe is shaped by patterns; from the stars in our galaxy to a snail's shell, a brick wall to the branches on trees, a bird's feather, the broccoli in your fridge, right down to ant holes and the little underworld they create in the soil, it's all mathematics and patterns, dear Watson! Your morning routine, the route you take to work, how you act and behave in front of different types of people, the way you brush your teeth and get dressed – it's all patterns! We are all constantly repeating patterns day in day out. The earliest humans evolved to see patterns everywhere because their survival was dependent on it. How else could they tell which berries were poisonous and which were safe to eat, and recognize signs of danger or other members of their tribe?

Our life patterns and familiar behaviours are usually a combination of genetic, environmental and subconscious conditioning passed down to us through the parenting we received as children. Monkey see, monkey do. Throughout our childhood, we took on the thoughts, attitudes, beliefs and patterns of our parents and then, in most cases, built lives similar to theirs. Many of our patterns help us get by. Without them, we'd forget to brush our teeth, how to drive a car, what train to jump on to get to work, when to pick the kids up from school, or what direction to pass the ball on the pitch! On the flip side, other patterns create chaos, keep us stuck or unhappy, because they're not really us, just behaviours we picked up and learnt along the way. It can be tricky to notice your patterns, because they go far deeper than the surface behaviours you repeat. Because we are wired to be habitual creatures, it is far easier for us to be controlled and made to conform. So if we really want to wake up and be free, then we have to break our personal patterns.

....

CONDITIONING: THE CARDS YOU ARE DEALT

In Southeast Asia, elephants are still used for transportation. At the end of each day, the elephant handlers prevent them from running away by looping a thin piece of rope round one of their legs and attaching it to the ground using a small stick. Do you think the elephants, capable of moving massive loads, couldn't simply pull out the stick and do a runner? Of course they could, so why don't they? When the elephants are young they are restrained by hefty ropes and no matter how hard they struggle and pull they can't escape. Over time they give up fighting and by the time they reach adulthood they have been conditioned to believe that they can't move when they're tied up, even though the smallest of tugs would set them free, so they stay trapped.

....

Like the elephant, our conditioning can also result in patterns that keep us stuck, so recognizing a pattern can be a transformational experience. It's like being trapped underwater for far too long and suddenly surfacing for air. That first gasp is life-saving! When you wake up and spot a pattern in your life and recognize your unwanted behaviours, it shifts your mind and you feel a lot lighter. The light bulb flashes and you feel like a dead weight has been lifted off your shoulders. But I've noticed that there's usually something else driving our unwanted behaviours and life patterns – usually unmet needs we are unaware of. For instance, some people eat emotionally, some smoke to relax or calm their nerves, others get high because they lack self-love, want to forget or want to feel connected. Yet no matter what the surface pattern might be or how frustrating and destructive the behaviour can get, there is always a deeper need in the driving seat. That's why we shouldn't judge others or ourselves for our behaviours and the patterns we repeat, we simply need to understand the underlying issue a lot more. Most people don't think this deeply and that's why they stay stuck doing things they hate for years.

We are much more than a bunch of unwanted habits and patterns.

AWARENESS, AWARENESS, AWARENESS

I'm guessing you've tried to change some of your behaviours in the past but they may have seemed impossible to change. Chances are that some of them feel so normal you think you can't stop repeating them no matter what you do. You may even feel that your patterns are now part of you; they've become your identity! The truth is we are not our behaviours, our brains have simply created a few internal programs to help us meet our deeper needs and prove that the beliefs we hold in our minds are correct. And so we can't stop repeating them no matter how many times we try.

You may have tried to change some of your behaviours in the past, but, before you knew it, slipped back into old, familiar patterns. Sometimes it can feel like you can't control yourself or stop repeating them. Maybe you were doing really well on a diet, or had broken some unhealthy addictions, or were having good fun in a relationship only for it to end the same way. Back to square one! When we're unaware of our patterns we keep repeating them. It doesn't matter who we meet, how proven the diet is, or how many years we stay clean, if there are some deeper needs driving our patterns and those needs are not met, it's just a matter of time until we slip up again.

One of my all-time spiritual heroes was a guy from India called Anthony de Mello. This dude was hilarious and mixed up deep truths and spiritual wisdom with lots of love and laughter – making awakening a pretty fun experience! He was a former Jesuit priest, psychologist, spiritual teacher and writer of one my favourite books, *Awareness* (read it and watch his videos out on YouTube if you want to be free from the madness). Anyway, one of the best takeaways I learnt from de Mello's teachings is his description of awareness: he wrote, '… until you became aware of something you keep doing, it controls you. But once you become aware of it, you control it.'

Awareness is key! If we don't investigate our underlying needs and discover what drives our patterns, then life can end up being an eternal Groundhog Day – repeating the same sh#t over and over again until we finally learn the lesson and get it right. Yet when we shine the light on our patterns, we see things more clearly. We take control and it's easier to break free from any negative patterns we might be repeating.

....

⊙ Zooming out

Grab your journal and put the heading 'PATTERNS' at the top of the page. Do it now! Remember, reading this book is only 5 per cent of your transformation; the other 95 per cent comes from you following these techniques and taking action.

Now spend a few minutes becoming aware of all the annoying patterns and habits that you keep repeating. Think about the behaviours that irritate you, upset you and frustrate you. Become aware and think about the patterns you feel you have no control over, keep repeating and could do without! Just write out a list of behaviours and patterns you repeat and would prefer not to.

Now zoom out and look at how long you've been repeating them. If you can't remember exactly, then take a wild guess!

Finally, take a look at each pattern and see how it may have affected your life and ask yourself:

* Where did this behaviour come from?

* How does it really make me feel?

* Who would I be without it?

* How would I feel once it's gone?

....

Like I said, when I look back to my early days of transformation, I was pretty hard on myself when I slipped up and fell into old patterns. I judged myself harshly and beat myself up with negative self-talk because I felt like I'd failed. But as soon as I tuned into my consciousness and my softer voice, I was able to coach myself through my slip-ups and see them as part of the process; they too were an opportunity to grow and learn something new about myself! In fact I learnt a lot more from my f#ck-ups than anything else!

Take my arrest for drink driving, again. I was gutted that one thoughtless decision, a lack of awareness and way too much tequila nearly cost me my life and my career. I felt like I was back at square one, but looking back now it was the best thing that ever happened to me. I needed to wake up to my beliefs and understand what was running the show at a deeper level. I had to meet my unmet needs in a more positive and productive way; otherwise I'd never have been able to break the cycle. So part of bringing awareness to your negative patterns is not judging yourself for them or beating yourself with negative self-talk when you slip up. Pick yourself up, dust yourself off, investigate why you hit repeat and learn from it before starting again!

ADDICTED TO PATTERNS

Your brain is addicted to the patterns you identified in the previous exercise. They are active and running programs inside your brain called beliefs. Your entire life is built around your belief system and what you believe is true. Your patterns and the behaviours you repeat in life are a reflection of two things: your beliefs and your unmet needs. So let's look at each in turn!

IDENTIFYING YOUR BELIEFS

Your beliefs are driving your actions and the behaviours you repeat. You may even wonder who you'd be without them? When we believe we are the sum total of our actions and behaviours, it can feel impossible to break the cycle. It's like believing we are our thoughts and the noise inside our heads! The truth is we're not a bunch of negative behaviours or unwanted patterns, our brains have simply created these programs to make life easier and to give us what we think we need.

Your beliefs are programmed in your mind at a subconscious level and they create the movie we discussed in Chapter 2. Beliefs are simply thoughts you've repeated over and over again for a number of years. Now you have an entire belief system lodged in your mind controlling your behaviours and trying to meet your needs. The hitch in the system is this: most of our beliefs are old, unhelpful and not needed any more. Some of them are false, myths we have either told ourselves or others have drilled into us at a young age. Here are some typically destructive and unhelpful beliefs my clients often hold:

* I'm worthless.
* I'm stupid.
* I never get it right.
* I'm not good enough.
* Nobody loves me.
* I'm a failure.
* It's their/my fault.
* The world is a dangerous place.
* Life is hard!

The brain transforms our invisible beliefs into recognizable behaviours. Our actions are basically proving our beliefs to be right. For instance, a person who is overweight might subconsciously believe that eating extra portions will make them feel whole, happy and satisfied in life. Someone who always sabotages their success might believe that they are stupid or a failure. Someone who sleeps around or has destructive and unhealthy relationships might believe they are worthless and unlovable so they put up with the abuse to try to satisfy the unmet need for love.

Underneath all negative behaviours there are negative beliefs running the show!

Repeating destructive behaviours reinforces the beliefs we hold to be true. It's a Catch-22! We act in ways we wished we didn't in an effort to meet our needs, but all we end up doing is strengthening the subconscious belief. Your surface behaviours are literally trying to match your deepest beliefs so you can prove that your belief system is right. Remember the Thinker and the Prover from pages 60–61? Well, this is the same process but on steroids!

Hand-me-down beliefs

The hardest beliefs to break away from are the ones passed down to us through the generations. Our parents unconsciously imprint their views, behaviours and patterns in very subtle ways onto our psyches. Over time they become ingrained in our minds so deeply that our parents' beliefs become ours. And their parents did the same to them! We're conditioned from the day we're born with hand-me-down beliefs. Good or bad, positive or negative, our beliefs affect how we show up in the world. We might be unaware of what was passed down to us, but we feel the consequences of our parents' beliefs every day of our lives. You might even find yourself re-enacting the same struggles and problems in life as your parents. For example, if you're a workaholic, you might realize it's damaging your health or feel torn apart at missing out on precious family time, but deeply believe that money equals success and so feel unable to stop. On the other hand, you might come from a similar background to mine in which you were subconsciously taught that money doesn't make you happy, you have to work hard to earn a penny, and chances are you'll never be successful or make it.

My parents never sat down and told me their beliefs; most parents don't, which is why they hand down their limiting beliefs. If parents did stop and check in with their own beliefs and give their kids a lesson on belief systems, then the parents would learn just as much as their children. This isn't a dig at parents, either – as I've said before, our parents do the best they can with what they know!

....

⊕ Recognizing family patterns

What patterns or behaviours do you find yourself repeating over and over that are similar to that of your parents'? Write them down and wake up to any hand-me-down beliefs. Are there issues about money, love, confidence, health, happiness, or maybe all of the above? Did your parents struggle with these patterns too?

Remember, this isn't about pointing the finger or blaming anyone, this is about pulling up the stick and setting yourself free. You might find that you are repeating patterns and holding on to beliefs that your parents believed were true, but have nothing to do with you and are the last thing you would ever think. The simple act of awareness and understanding your parents' beliefs and behaviours can put you back in the driving seat of your own life!

IDENTIFYING DEEPER NEEDS

I've described earlier how all our behaviours and patterns are trying to meet underlying needs within us so, in order to break our patterns, we usually have to fill that hole, or replace a negative pattern with a positive one. We need to meet each need with a more positive behaviour, which I like to think of as filling ourselves up from the inside out. Don't worry, I'm not going to get too spiritual on your ass. Let's keep it simple!

After 10 years of working with clients, I've recognized the problems they present with are never really the real problem. Their problems are an illusion. Let me explain. Many people seek help because they're eager to change their life. They might be unaware of their patterns and underlying needs, but are frustrated with unwanted behaviours because they're zapping their power and holding them back in life. So we jump on Skype and they talk about their issue, but they're usually a million miles away from the true underlying dilemma that is driving their behaviours and wrecking their life.

An obvious example is a heroin addict. Injecting gear is a pretty horrific pattern, right? But it's still an illusion: injecting heroin is only the surface problem we can see. Yes, there are patterns now firing off in the brain and chemicals buzzing around. However, deep down, in the non-tangible realm of feelings and unmet needs, the drug user will have underlying needs that are driving their behaviour. In my experience, 95 per cent of heroin users lacked love, were abused or felt abandoned and rejected at a young age so they take smack because they are using either to numb out the pain and trauma or to fill what I call 'a hole in the soul'. Even if heroin is destroying their lives, they will do anything for a fix of warmth, comfort and connection. Even if it's an illusion and only lasts for a brief moment!

If you don't understand the needs that are driving your unwanted behaviours, then it will feel impossible to break them and create new, empowering ones. I spent a few years investigating my own patterns and behaviours. I needed to know why I acted in certain ways and what needs I was really trying to meet. I knew I wasn't a bad person, no kid puts his or her hand up at school when the teacher asks what they want to be when they are older and announces, 'I want to take drugs and commit crime, Miss.'

As you know, I'm all for getting on with it, living in the now and creating a vision, plus I have many wild and wacky tools to help you transform, but if you don't know what's going on at a deeper level then it will bite you on the butt and trip you up along the way. I needed to know why I found so much comfort in drugs and alcohol, and why I couldn't stop until I was unconscious. When I understood my unmet needs, I was able to meet them more positively and break the unwanted patterns that led me astray. For me it was all about love, I needed to fill myself up from the inside and truly love this hunky fella 100 per cent! As I looked more deeply, I realized I had low self-worth, a lack of real confidence and didn't know who I was because I wore so many masks.

If you don't know why you do what you do, then chances are you'll repeat negative patterns for the rest of your life. So let's dig a little deeper and release some of this crap that's not serving you.

⊕ **Discover your hidden needs**

Take a look at the list of behaviours and patterns you wrote out in the previous exercise. Now I want you to become like Sherlock Holmes and do some detective work. For each pattern you listed, ask yourself the following questions:

* What's driving this pattern?
* What's underneath this behaviour?
* Why am I really repeating it?
* What need am I trying to meet?
* What are my beliefs about this behaviour?

Take one pattern at a time, close your eyes and connect to it. I often have little pattern epiphanies where I recognize my behaviours when I'm relaxed and getting Zen on a yoga mat. So relax, take it easy and get to know yourself and your patterns at a deeper level.

Once you become aware of the patterns, and the needs driving them, start thinking about how you could meet those needs more authentically by changing your behaviours. When you discover what you are really seeking deep within you, honour it and fulfill that need as genuinely as you can. Otherwise you'll be trying to meet needs with harmful and unwanted patterns for a very long time. In my case, I had to face myself in the mirror and speak in a more loving way to myself. (More on that in Chapter 8!)

BREAKING PATTERNS

When you interrupt your behaviours and change your unwanted patterns, you cut short the programs looping inside your brain and begin to break the circuit inside your subconscious mind. This sends a signal back to your brain that something new is taking place and that the old pattern is not needed any more. The more you face your behaviours, the easier it is to break the patterns. Breaking patterns can feel uncomfortable when you first look within and begin this process, but when you see the results showing up in your life you'll want to do it more and more. You'll look forward to breaking the rest of the negative habits that might be destroying your bliss!

Now you've become more aware of your patterns, use the following four-step process to help smash through them one by one. Take one pattern at a time from the list you created earlier and work through the steps below. I've used this process a number of times to help me gain more awareness about the destructive behaviours in my life – from stopping drinking to exercising, freeing myself from debt to writing this book. This four-step process can work with any pattern you want to break!

#1 TIMELINE YOUR PATTERN

First pick one pattern that you want to break. Think how long you've been repeating it and where it started. Grab a piece of paper and on the left-hand side put the date it started. Then notice when you've experienced it throughout your life by time lining it. In other words, list all the times and places you've repeated it and work your way to the present day. Put a day or write a word on your timeline, for each time this pattern came up in your life.

You might also want to write down why you think it came up each time. Where were you? Who where you with? What do you think triggered it? How did it make you feel when you repeated it? Simply recognize the life span of your patterns and how you were feeling and what you were thinking each time you repeated them. See if you can spot any similarities between the times your pattern took over. Did you feel powerless, out of control, or was there something deeper driving it? Find any connections linked to each event, time or place you repeated this behaviour.

#2 IDENTIFY YOUR SIDs

SID is an acronym for the 'seemingly irrelevant decisions' we make that keep us stuck in our patterns. I learnt this at the drop-in centre where I used to volunteer. Your SIDs give your patterns life and if you want to break a pattern then you need to trace the SIDs that you make before you act out and repeat the pattern. For example, you don't get drunk when you're in the pub, you get drunk when you make the decision to go to the pub. You don't cheat on your girlfriend when you're caught with your pants down, you cheat when you start texting someone and making arrangements to meet in a hotel. And you don't get fat on one cheeky takeaway, you put on the pounds when you choose not to go to the gym and you eat out every night. Every day we make SIDs and never really pay them much attention.

This step might sound obvious, but it's so easy to trip up on the SIDs that we make over and over again. You can only break your pattern by becoming aware of the first and earliest decision you make before you even step into the situation or trigger your negative behaviour.

For the pattern you just timelined, trace back to the SIDs that you made before you acted out and gave it life. When you become aware of your SIDs, you train your brain to begin to notice the impulsive choices you make way before you repeat unwanted patterns. You can then talk yourself out of it and the pattern naturally disappears. In this way you build up your inner strength to say no, to respond positively and to choose not to make the decision.

#3 REPLACE YOUR PATTERNS

When we take something away from ourselves or try to stop repeating a pattern, then we must replace it with something positive, otherwise we'll feel like there's a void – an unmet need. For example, if you want to combat late-night chocolate cravings, then you'll need to be ready to replace the chocolate with plenty of tasty, healthy snacks that you chose the last time you went shopping. By doing this, you still meet the need but without falling into a negative pattern. Whether it's chocolate or crack, think of something you can put in its place to help you break the cycle!

Take a look at the pattern you timelined and write down some new actions and activities that could replace it. For example, when to get myself out of debt, I cut up my credit cards and only took out the cash I needed. That way, I knew exactly how much I was spending and only bought what I needed rather than random, impulse purchases I didn't need.

#4 VISUALIZE YOUR SUCCESS

You learned about the power of visualization in and how it can radically transform your life in Chapter 3. Now it's time to use your imagination to create even more successful outcomes and stop yourself falling back into old patterns. Look at the list of new pattern replacements you've just decided to make instead of the SIDs.

Now close your eyes and spend a few minutes creating a movie in your mind, seeing yourself making these new choices. See yourself walking right up to your old pattern, and then just before you act it out replacing it with your new action. Make the colours bigger and brighter. Feel great about taking control of your life and staying in control!

See yourself turn the other way, then see yourself free of the old pattern and enjoying the success of your new actions. For instance, you might feel stronger, more confident, happier and more excited about the new choices you've just made. With your eyes closed, watch yourself in your mind's eye making the new choices over and over again, saying no, turning the other way and following through with your action.

CREATE NEW PATTERNS: TAKE 30 DAYS

Of course, when we understand our SIDs we have to take action. There's no point in recognizing your patterns and repeating them. That is insanity! You'll end up feeling even more frustrated with yourself. As soon as you see your SIDs, you'll get to know yourself at a deeper level, you'll have more awareness, so follow through by making the right choices – otherwise, it will do your nut in!

Studies in neuroscience suggest that it takes 21 days for the brain to rewire and shape new pathways and break old habits. In my personal experience, it can take up to 30 days for a new pattern to become second nature. You already have a list of unhelpful patterns, so start off with a small one. Think of a pattern you want to break and then think about what you can put in place of it. For example, if you want to stop eating junk food, focus on filling the house with healthy food and empty it of everything else, take a 10-minute jog or walk around the block after work or dinner, spend 10 minutes in meditation for relaxation. Don't focus on quitting junk food, focus on what you want instead – being healthier – and bring a few new images of what this looks like to mind.

Be aware of the old patterns you want to break, understand why you do what you do, and what drives you, and then put every bit of energy you have into creating your new patterns. Remember, energy flows where attention goes. If you think it's too hard to get healthy, quit smoking, give up the booze or make more money, then you'll prove yourself right. On the flip side, if you focus on a few new patterns, learn how to raise your vibration and feel good for the next 30 days, your life will transform quicker than you can imagine. Creating new patterns will be easy and the epic vision you created for the future will get closer.

LIFE LESSONS

Spiritually speaking, I believe we all have life lessons to master. These are huge patterns that we came here to learn and seem to repeat until we understand the lesson, then they disappear as though by magic and we feel freer. Life has a funny way of teaching us our lessons too. They may come disguised as problems that keep hitting us hard, when we are at rock bottom or a crossroads in life.

Life lessons help us grow and become who we are!

When we overcome our lessons in life, something greater emerges. They show us what we need to learn, let go of, or work through. The same situation, event or person will keep coming into our lives over and over again until we learn the lesson behind it. If you have bouts of depression, then you may need to learn the life lesson of caring for yourself more and finding your purpose in life. Someone who sleeps around may need to learn the lesson of self-love and self-respect, while another who dreams big but procrastinates may need to learn the lesson of discipline and focus.

Our life lessons are personal; only you can dig deep and discover them, and they can take a whole lifetime to master. Usually these lessons are the complete opposite of whatever it is we are struggling with. The struggle seems to be the guide, the rock bottom is the gift, and the journey is achieving the complete opposite to what we know. Those who hate themselves and feel uncomfortable in their skin may need to learn the lesson of self-love; those with bitter and jealous attitudes towards others who succeed may need to learn how to be happy for others and separate from their ego; those who are constantly taking from life but feel empty may need to learn the lesson of giving!

Nobody else really cares whether you take this journey or not. It's between you and you!

◉ Digging deeper for your life lessons

Use this quick exercise to help you start to understand the life lessons contained within each of your patterns. Remember; life lessons are just bigger patterns you repeat over a longer period of time, often years. Answer the questions below about any or all of the negative patterns you repeat:

* If I could guess, what are my life lessons?
* What will I learn from these life lessons?
* How will my lessons transform my life?
* What will be the benefits when I overcome them?
* Who will be benefit when I learn my lessons?
* What's my first step now?

Of course your family and friends might worry that you're out of control, but it's only you who will truly suffer by repeating the same lesson (bigger patterns) over and over again. There are no shortcuts overcoming your life lessons either; learning them is key to creating life's epic adventure.

Think of it this way: your life lessons are gifts in disguise. The drug addict who gets clean finds true happiness, the guy who stops sleeping around and buying fast cars builds his self-esteem and will love himself so much that he'll find the perfect partner, the stress head in the city may finally find true inner peace and tranquillity when he or she realizes there is more to life than work. Some life lessons are deeper than others and may span a number of years. Some people spend a whole lifetime unaware of their lessons and never understand them.

Really spend some time on this one. Use a blank page to answer each question and dig deeper.

CHAPTER 6

ENGINEERING YOUR ENERGY

'THE ULTIMATE MEASURE OF OUR LIVES IS NOT HOW MUCH TIME WE SPEND ON THE PLANET, BUT RATHER HOW MUCH ENERGY WE INVEST IN THE TIME THAT WE HAVE.'

Jim Loehr and Tony Schwartz, *The Power of Full Engagement*

7 JUNE 2010

'Brett, take this instead of the money I owe you.'

My hand automatically opened up and reached out. As soon as the wrap landed in my palm, my belly did a somersault with excitement and my body tingled with a naughty buzz that I hadn't felt in years. I'd been off the booze and drugs for three years – I'd given up after my last escapade landed me in Woking police station. Luckily, the judge took into account all the hard work I had put in over the years and saw how I was trying to change my life. He even gave me some wisdom and told me to keep going: 'Stay on the path, Mr Moran, and don't let this drag you back, you're doing well and it takes time to change.' I was given a five-year driving ban instead of another sentence.

But now I was in Ibiza, miles away from Woking, and the nightlife was buzzing! I was at a local bar with some mates. The house music was pumping from every direction. People looked loved up on music and drugs. Half-naked women walked up and down the lanes promoting epic clubs and flashing their tits. It was our first night out and the pressure was already on me!

I swiftly stashed the three pills and a gram of MDMA powder in my jeans pocket. The f#ck-it switch was flicked and I was straight back where I left off three years ago. My chest pounded. My legs felt jittery and without thinking I jumped off my stool and headed straight to the toilets. I dashed into a cubicle and locked the door behind me. Feeling anxious, my stomach got tighter and I needed a sh#t from all the nerves. I hadn't taken a pill or MDMA powder in a long time and I loved them both!

Like an eager kid opening Christmas presents, I unwrapped the little gift and felt hypnotized by the glistening MDMA rocks. The mini pile of artificial utopia looked potent and I knew the buzz would be strong and powerful. For some reason, before I dabbed it, I stopped, looked up and caught sight of my reflection in the mirror. I looked into my eyes and started mindfully breathing through the physical cravings and all the anxiety whizzing around in my body.

'Brett, you don't need it, mate. You don't do this any more. Remember your vow!' My inner guru had packed his bags and flown to Ibiza with me! I could feel him in my core and heard his voice loud and clear!

After my last drink-driving offence and lucky escape, I'd travelled to Thailand and stayed with the Buddhist monks. Instead of hitting the go-go bars and smoking yabba, I'd stayed at a temple called Thamkrabok, done some chanting, taken a crazy detox and started a five-year year *Satja* (vow) not to drink alcohol or touch drugs. Standing alone in the cubicle, every cell in my body craved the drugs in my hand. My vow almost went out of the window!

The devil on my shoulder screamed at me to swallow the pills and take a little dab in the powder. Then a louder voice spoke up and told me not to do it. As I stood in the toilet, staring in the mirror with the wrap in my hand, and a battle going on inside my head, I felt the conflict sucking my night away!

'Just give it back, Brett. Say thanks but no thanks. You'll be gutted tomorrow if you don't and it won't end here. It never does!'

So said the little angel perched on my shoulder.

'*Is this a test?*' I thought. '*Am I supposed to say no? Is God or the Buddha watching over me in bloody Ibiza? Or maybe that's a load of bollocks and it's time to get smashed! Just take the pills, Brett, don't drink. It'll be fine!*'

I unwrapped the parcel a bit more and my hands started to clam up with sweat. The devil reminded me of the energy and fun times ecstasy had given me and didn't say anything about the comedowns. '*You're not addicted any more, Brett. You can handle it. Just take one pill. What's the worst that can happen?*'

My true self came straight back. '*Brett, you don't need it! You can have a great night without it. Think where it will end. You're stronger than this. Give it back!*'

For a moment I watched my mind battle with itself and took a back seat. Then all of a sudden, like Sherlock Holmes solving a mystery in Baker Street, my mind fast-forwarded and I imagined how I'd feel the next day. I envisioned my comedown, I saw how bad I would end up, and I felt how awful I would feel. I saw myself looking totally wrecked and broken! It felt horrible just thinking about it. I knew how it would end up. Once I popped I never stopped! Some people know when to stop. When enough is enough, they can say no, but not me, I have some self-destructive entity within me that wants me to suffer. It would never have stopped at one pill – I would have been taking drugs on the plane home. F#ck, I would have been trying to fly the plane!

I turned on the tap and splashed my face with cold water. After what seemed like a lifetime of standing in the tiny cubicle, I wrapped the little parcel up again, stuffed it back in my pocket and smiled in the mirror. *'You don't need it mate, you've got this!'* I walked back outside and placed the wrap back in my mate's hand, 'No thanks. I don't need it. Give me my money tomorrow.'

After we finished our drinks we headed for Pacha, one of Ibiza's best clubs! Everyone was high on something, except me. And I never wanted any of it! I felt alive naturally and the music was inside me. For once I was in control and it felt good to finally say no to my inner demons. My energy was buzzing and I felt euphoric for the first time – and without any artificial chemicals whizzing around in my system. I danced until 6 a.m. and lost count of the number of people who approached me asking for pills, coke – whatever I was on. When I told them I was sober and drinking water, they looked at me in disbelief. I was so high on life that I looked off my face!

ENERGY: THAT EPIC HIGH THAT MAKES YOU FEEL ALIVE!

Who doesn't want to feel energized, enthusiastic and have more oomph in their daily lives? Activating our energy gives us the zest we're all looking for. It keeps the fire in our belly ignited and makes us feel alert. If you want to boost your moods, balance your health and feel more joy, then engineering your energy is a must. Knowing how to look after it makes us feel more positive and productive and we wake up in the morning feeling eager and passionate about getting started. By choosing to make this inner buzz, we really can ignite a volcano of energy erupt within us. For most people it's simply waiting to happen, but they don't know how to unlock it naturally or look after it, so they feel flat and their inner volcano stays dormant.

Now you're making changes to propel yourself towards your vision, you're going to need all the energy you can get. This pure natural stimulant is living right inside you and once you engineer it, you can rocket fuel your life. After all, having more energy, feeling more alive and active is what gives you that extra kick. It's what puts you into a higher vibration and makes it easier to attract what you want, which in turn helps you stay motivated to create the life you dream about. So why wouldn't we want more of this natural buzz!

After that night in Ibiza I realized that I had the buzz within me and since then I have had many more nights like Pacha. Some have been so pure and exhilarating that I felt like I wanted to explode! Every cell in my body vibrates at some extreme velocity and I feel like I'm going to burst with joy. I know anyone can tap into such an incredible sensation without taking any external stimulant or pick-me-up. But if you had told me a decade ago I could feel this high on life without having to drink, snort or swallow something, I would have called you a nut job and laughed in your face.

After learning how to engineer my energy and showing my clients how to ignite this epic rush within them, I noticed that this inner spark is always within us; even if we feel flat and like the light inside has gone out, it's still there. All we need to do is tune into it and learn how to ignite it more organically. The more we take care of this inner natural buzz, the higher we go!

RESERVOIRS OF ENERGY

Engineering energy is a lot like digging for oil. We can't see it on the surface, but dig deep enough and there's an abundance of it waiting for us. The problem we face, just like Mother Earth, is that society is bleeding us dry. Just like sucking the oil out of the earth, the societies we live in seems to be sucking the energy out of the human race and we can't keep up with the rate any more! We know that one day the planet's sources of oil will be exhausted, so we are already we're working on finding new resources to keep civilization going and things ticking over for future generations. Solar panels, cars that run on hydrogen, and I'm sure there's going to be a lot more creative inventions coming our way in the next 20 years or so. However, what happens when your personal energy runs out and you feel drained, when you abuse it because you're trying to keep up with the rat race and you burn out with exhaustion. How do you fix that?

ZAPPED!

I know what you might be thinking because I hear it all the time from my clients – how on Earth can you ignite more energy and power when you feel flat, tired and stressed out? When you're working your socks off or when you have toddlers to look after and hardly any time for yourself! I get it. But first things first, remember that everything in life is a choice. If your energy is low because you're burning the candle at both ends and the demands of life are getting on top of you, then you need to make some new choices, otherwise you'll always be running on empty.

There's no denying that the demands of life can knock us out of sync with our natural energy rhythms. We work longer hours, have less time to rest, perhaps do two jobs just to pay the bills, grab fast food on the go, catch up on sleep at the weekends if we're lucky, and our bodies ache and feel stiff because we don't have time to relax. It's not unusual to take sleeping pills to switch off at night, or to boost our days with caffeine, sugar and a cocktail of other artificial stimulants just to get through it. Or to dabble with narcotics on the weekends so we can feel something greater than the mundane numbness.

When you stop and look around you, you will see that the majority of people are racing through life on empty, feeling exhausted, burnt out and rarely pausing to connect to and nurture the energy within. I've seen young teenagers overworked in coffee shops with black bags under their eyes, stressed-out mums feeling guilty because they need a break from the kids, and zombies walking into the office every Monday morning because they're trying to keep up with the race and have ignored life's most precious asset. Not only are our energy levels being sucked dry, but we also end up losing precious time with our families when we lack the oomph and drive to connect. We find it hard to switch off or reflect on where we're going in life because our days are filled with playing catch up or wondering why we feel deflated and lifeless. And when we feel tired, our thoughts become more negative and our feelings become heavier, we lose passion for our vision and fall back into the more harmful patterns.

It's not just a crazy work–life balance that throws our energy levels out of sync either, it's also the foods we eat and how well we choose to look after these epic spacesuits that we live in. What we put into our system affects everything, from our energy to our drive, our health to our happiness, and our motivation to our success. So if you lack the energy to jump out of bed in the morning, you're always trying to play catch up and ignoring the aches and pains in your precious body, then you might crash and burn and seize up way before your time. On the other hand, if you want to tap into this insane reservoir of energy and really ignite your health so you feel high on life and buzzing on pureness, get more done, and recharge daily as you charge towards your vision, then making a few subtle shifts in your lifestyle and taking better care of your energy is key.

To optimize your energy and get the maximum benefits from it, you also need to use it in the most efficient way possible. Don't waste it on stuff that doesn't excite you if it's draining your energy. Just because everyone else is doing it, that doesn't mean it's normal! Instead, become a master of your energy and use it wisely on things that you love doing – playing with the kids, working out, going on adventures or meditating on your mat.

Use your energy doing the things you love doing.

⊙ Evaluating your energy

The following seven questions will help you determine your overall energy levels and the areas in your life that you need to focus on the most:

* When I wake up in the morning I usually feel . . .
* My weight makes me feel . . .
* My daily energy is . . .
* My sleeping patterns make me feel . . .
* When I get home from work I feel . . .
* My stress levels are . . .
* My mind set is usually . . .

Only you can answer whether you feel full of energy and vitality, or low and sluggish. Whether you jump out of bed with a spring in your step or wish you could sleep all day. It's only you who's going to crash and burn every few weeks or months and feel like you can't cope. So are you too busy to think about your energy and health or is now the time to do something about it?

....

GETTING HIGH ON LIFE

If you want to feel this inner buzz, then you need to take care of number one. Keep your energy clean and you'll ignite it more naturally and organically. Rather then being up one minute and crashing the next, you'll find a natural ebb and flow and enjoy the buzz a lot more. As your energy becomes more balanced so do your moods and emotions, your thoughts seem a lot cleaner and calmer too. Of course we all need to recharge once in a while, but once you learn how to recharge your energy naturally your energy levels sky rocket. You'll tap into the pure force within you and have more get-up-and-go to play with the kids, work later or party harder (see you in Ibiza!). You don't need any pick-me-ups to boost you or get you through the day once you master this inner power!

....

◉ Natural highs

If you're feeling zapped then I don't need to tell you it's time to do something about it and get your power back. You're smart, you already know what to do, but sometimes we just need that gentle reminder.

Grab your journal and write down all the things that pick you up, excite you, make you feel high, happy, in the zone and alive (this is not coffee, energy drinks, pills, sugar, cake,

spending money or any form of drugs – natural highs only).
Think about all the activities you used to take pleasure in, simple
stuff that made you feel energized and really connected.

For example, you might include:

* A walk in nature or taking the dog for a walk

* A relaxing bath with candles

* Meditation, yoga, or some form of exercise

* Dancing, football or tennis

* Playtime with the kids

* Reading, writing, painting or any other creative activity

* Making love in a passionate way (sexual energy is epic!)

Pick one activity from your list and choose to do it at least three
times this week, then make a note of how you feel and how your
energy levels are at the end of the week. For instance, you could
have a warm bath and get an early night every night instead of
watching late-night TV or a film on Netflix. You could wake up
and energize yourself by doing a 20-minute yoga practice or
meditation in the morning before starting your day. Or you could
get some fresh air and walk around the local park and connect
to nature with the kids and really ignite your energy. Do it for a
week and see how different you feel.

WIPED OUT AND DISCONNECTED

I guess what can be harder to recognize than feeling a little low and
flat from time to time is when you lose your spark and your get-up-
and-go for life in general. You feel disconnected from the source
of your energy and lack the drive to do anything. A number of my

private clients come to me because they feel like they have lost their inner spark and life has taken over. They have either neglected or abused their inner system or not paid any attention to their natural resources. A lot of people who do this seem to think they can just keep going and play catch up their whole lives. Perhaps they can, but why bother when there is a much easier way?

Here are some of the problems I've heard over the years:

* I lack enthusiasm for life
* I feel irritated with loved ones and self
* I get impatient with loved ones and self
* I have lost interested in things I used to enjoy
* I have heavy, dense emotions
* I feel old before my time
* I have foggy, cloudy thoughts
* I am tired and fatigued most days
* I feel withdrawn instead of connecting, feeling motivated and alive
* I suffer from long-term depression

Do you see yourself in any of these? Admittedly, we all feel a little under par from time to time and lack some oomph, but if you encounter any of the above on a regular basis then it's time to make some big changes. Life isn't meant to be this way, we are here to thrive and feel alive, not feel flat and depressed.

People end up feeling this way when they lack energy. For some, life seems consistently flat and they can't imagine feeling any other way, so they reach for the artificial fixes, pop the pills and never reach out for help. If you know you've lost your drive but brush the thought aside, go to work and get on with things and sleep in your spare time, then life can often become more about clock watching, counting down the days in the week and just getting through the day. We all know this isn't a life that is going to give us the edge we want. This is not going to tune us into the bliss, turn our vision into reality. Life can become soul-destroying when we live this way and choose not to do anything about it.

Feeling flat and lacking energy is a sign that you need to wake the f#ck up and ask yourself, what's more important than enjoying my life?

No doubt you already know where you'd like your energy levels to be. I'm hoping you can't wait to tap into this inner pool of energy and really take control of your life.

SEVEN KEYS TO IGNITING YOUR ENERGY

Creating highly effective energy is the way forward if you want more from life. That doesn't mean we have to aim to be like the Duracell bunny on speed. I've had rushes of energy explode through my body while I'm sitting on my yoga mat feeling very calm and Zen. This energy doesn't always have to be high-octane but it's always alive! Inside you. Igniting energy means you can tap into this deeper reservoir when you need it and you can feel this almighty river gushing through your body like the Niagara Falls. The seven keys below will help you purify, maintain and ignite surges of energy. The last one will show you how to kick-start your energy instantly and really tune into this inner magic.

#1 START WITH YOUR MINDSET

It's important to de-stress and set your mind up for positivity as soon as you open your eyes. If you're lucky you may notice a moment of silence before your mind starts wandering and you think about your to-do list and the day ahead. For most people, however, the mind will become active with racing thoughts or worries before they're even fully awake. Each morning, take a few moments to relax and remind yourself that you are not your thoughts.

Asking yourself a few positive questions in the morning can really set your day up too. They shift your focus and activate your energy. The following questions wire a positive and calm mindset into your brain every morning:

* What have I achieved in my life already?
* What excites me about my future?
* What am I proud of in my life?
* What am I grateful for?
* What do I need to let go of to create more peace and happiness?

#2 GET MORE SLEEP

While we're in bed relaxing, let's remember how important sleep is to our health, mood and energy. Lack of sleep can affect your whole day. Nowadays it's all too easy to read emails, catch up on Facebook notifications or watch TV instead of just going to sleep. Getting more sleep gives you more energy, makes the day ahead seem easier and recharges your mind and body optimally. Here are six tips to get a decent night's kip and keep your energy charged though the day:

* Stop watching TV and turn off your computer an hour before bedtime.
* Spend some time reading before switching off the light.
* Get at least eight hours of sleep every night.
* Wake up and drink a glass of water.
* Meditate, stretch or visualize before you get out of bed.
* Don't check your phone or email until you are out of bed and are ready for the day.

#3 TAKE A SOCIAL MEDIA DETOX

I don't know about you, but if I sit at a screen too long I start to feel zapped because the pixels on your screen actually suck your energy and mental activity, so I do my best to mix it up a bit. A few hours on the Mac, then I have a break and take a walk or do a quick meditation. Just a 10-minute break every hour during your working day will help you rebalance your energy. Or delete the Facebook app from your phone and just check in once a day. Not only does this boost your energy levels, but it also catapults your productivity levels too! Or if you're brave enough, give yourself a break at the weekend and stay offline and notice the increase in your energy levels on Monday morning.

#4 HYDRATE YOUR ENERGY

The number one 'natural' energy booster has to be good old H_2O. Who would have believed that plain water could boost your energy! Not only that, but it's the best way to purify your system – the body is made up of 80 per cent water, the brain 85 per cent. Most people who feel drained and fatigued are probably struggling due to dehydration. What's more, we often confuse feeling peckish and feeling thirsty. By drinking more water you not only boost your energy and balance, but your body will actually lose excess belly fat because drinking water quenches your thirst and stops hunger pangs.

So how much water do you drink? That's the million-dollar question. Most experts suggest drinking about two litres of water a day. But if that's a big jump from where you are right now, just double your water intake and take it from there. I started off by placing a big glass of water by on the bedside table before going to bed each night. Soon as I woke up I necked it back and it created a new pattern.

#5 DETOX YOUR BODY

We all know that alcohol is poison for the body and that a hangover can make us feel like death warmed up. A good old binge can leave us feeling groggy and cloudy at best, or low and depressed for days. I'm not suggesting that you stop drinking altogether, how dare I! But if you drink every day, a few times a week or use alcohol to relax or help you sleep, then just reduce your intake and see what happens. Replace that pattern with something more positive and stick to it as you monitor how you feel and your levels of energy.

While we're on the subject, Class As are not going to help anyone improve their energy or health either. If you're using drugs then I'd suggest you see an addiction specialist or hit me up to get the support you need to quit. But other drugs, such as painkillers, sleeping tablets and nicotine are just as bad. Another stimulant to be aware of is caffeine which for many people is part of their daily routine. Just pay attention to how much you're drinking and how it affects your energy, moods and emotions. Be aware that caffeine is just as addictive as cocaine and has some serious side effects too. It raises your blood pressure, so if you have a weak ticker it could be damaging it in the long run. Caffeine can also trigger feelings of anxiety, interfere with your sleep patterns, disrupt your natural energy cycles and have a negative effect on your overall happiness. Enough said.

#6 EAT FOR ENERGY

Did you know your diet is affecting your energy too? Colourful fruits and vegetables have a lighter, higher vibration because they are alive and energetic, while fatty, greasy or sugary foods and meat have a lower vibration because they are dense and dead. Whatever you choose to put in your body will affect you in the short term and in the long term. I'm not saying you have to become a vegetarian and fill the fridge with broccoli and watermelon (even though they are super healthy and you will feel high on energy), but making a few small adjustments in your overall diet is key to waking your energy up and feeling higher then Snoop Dogg! (Minus the skunk!) Below are four ways you can optimize your diet:

Start juicing

Just one juice in the morning will boost your mood and energy! Think about it, when you down a glass of carrot, cucumber or broccoli juice all that goodness shoots around your body and sends all the nutrients to your vital organs. Make sure you whack some superfoods, such as goji berries, broccoli or spirulina in your juice to give you that extra charge. One thing I'm addicted to in the mornings is an apple and ginger shot. It kick-starts my day and makes my energy buzz! It's the new tequila!

Eat your fruit and veg

Do your best to eat at least five portions of fruit and vegetables a day.

Eat them as snacks and it will stop you from bingeing and diving into the cookie jar or stopping by the vending machine and handing over your energy to the candy man! Increase the variety of fruits and veg too, so that you're eating a rainbow of colours to get the optimum balance of fibre and nutrients to fuel your body and feel epic!

Eat smaller portions

Have you ever asked yourself who made up the portion size on our plate? Did you know in Thailand and other Asian countries they eat four to five times a day but in much smaller portions? If you want to feel energized and lose weight then reduce your portion sizes. Being a yogi there are days when I only eat two small portions or just have a few juices. Especially when I'm on retreat, I find my body just doesn't need as much food. Years ago I'd stuff my face, feel fat and bloated and wonder why my energy was low.

Eat less meat

I've found that eating animal products negatively affects my mind, moods and emotions. Like I said, all food is energy and has a conscious vibration. If you want to ignite your spark, feel a lot lighter, happier and more in the zone, then give meat a break. Just cut back every now and then or choose to have two to three days of the week when you don't eat any meat.

#7 TAKE A COLD SHOWER

If you want to feel instantly energized then turn the cold tap on and jump under the shower. A few years ago I spent over £2k on a course to learn about online marketing. The last thing I was expecting was someone telling me to take cold showers and stop eating meat for

30 days! I thought my mentor was insane, but I wanted more energy, focus, success and productivity so I gave it a go.

Taking a cold shower is hands down the best energy and mood booster I have ever experienced! As soon as the cold water hits your body you feel energetic, alert and alive – and frozen! Some days I even had two because I wanted more energy in the evening. Try it yourself, I dare you! Cold showers are also great for helping you break negative moods, stop cravings and can lift depression.

You have the greatest reservoir of energy within you, but you need to activate it!

It seems to me more and more people are waking up and going back to basics. I recently rented a remote cottage out in nature; I had no TV, no Internet connection. I ate my dinner outside, went for long walks. When we step out of the virtual world and reconnect to the real world, we feel deeply connected, energetic and yup, you guessed it . . . ALIVE!

⊕ The 30-day challenge

I'm going to call you out and challenge you to add a few of the above to your daily routine. The changes don't have to be permanent, just for 30 days and then, if you want, you can go straight back to how you were before. So here's the challenge.

* Next time you go shopping, stock up on more fruit and vegetables.
* Invest in a cheap juicer or smoothie maker and replace your morning coffee with a delicious juice or smoothie.
* Turn off your computer and any mobile devices an hour before bedtime.
* Wake up and do some light yoga, stretching or meditation before starting your day.
* Hold back on the meat, caffeine, fizzy drinks and alcohol.
* Drink more water.

How simple is that! The idea is to go for 30 days and cleanse your mind and body so you can improve your health and monitor how you feel and your energy levels. For 30 days take note of your entire journey, write about it in your journal and see what thoughts you think, how you feel and what your energy is like. Be aware that during the first week your mind will be all over the place, it will do everything within its sneaky power to fool you into pigging out, eating junk food or watching films late at night or resisting yoga and meditation in the morning. This is natural, your mind and body is just going through a cleansing process, don't give in to the cravings, stay focused and remember why you want to feel healthy and have more energy.

THE YOGA REVOLUTION

Yoga is epic! And it's sweeping the world as millions of people are waking up, getting Zen and joining the yoga revolution. Yoga is so much more than standing tall on your mat or doing handstands for Instagram. It reveals a deeper aspect of your self, connects you to a greater energy and makes something inside you come alive. As you go deeper, your body loosens up, your emotions calm, your aches and pains fade away and your mind becomes so clear.

Any kind of exercise can work wonders for our energy levels. For starters, exercise increases serotonin levels, which means the body produces more of the feel-good endorphins that can help us feel more peaceful, balanced and happy. Serotonin is a chemical created by the body that works as a neurotransmitter and is believed to be responsible for maintaining your positive moods. A shortage of serotonin can lead to feeling low and depressed, and so the more serotonin you engineer by exercising, the happier you will feel.

In clinical trials yoga is shown not only to increase your levels of serotonin and other 'happy' chemicals in the brain, but also engineers your consciousness and helps you become more mindful, relaxed and present. To me, yoga ticks all the boxes. It's a great workout, a spiritual practice, plus it gives us timeout from the fast-paced society we live in.

For me yoga creates a deeper connection to the mind, body breath and spirit. I'm not sure what it is about yoga and breathing more deeply and intentionally, but it takes you out of the madness and you see things more clearly. Yoga isn't new, it has been around for thousands of years. In Hinduism and Buddhism the word yoga means 'spiritual discipline', which points to the fact that it's not just about physical exercise, but also mindfulness, relaxation, breathing, diet, positive action and, of course, meditation, which all enhance energy, health and happiness.

Yoga is a way of life that can put you in touch with your higher self, open your heart fully and ignite insane levels of energy!

⊕ Bend your body

For some, yoga becomes a way of life, but you don't need to be a long-bearded guru sitting cross-legged in a cave, draped in prayer beads, wearing skimpy Speedos and humming 'Om' all day and night to join the yoga revolution. You can practise at home watching YouTube, in the park, hit a few studios or join me at one of my retreats. Every day more people are choosing to bend their bodies and get Zen, because no matter what your current level of fitness, how big or small you are, what you weigh, or whether you're into yoga's more spiritual aspects or not, everyone is welcome and everyone can feel the benefits of awakening in yoga if they keep to it. If going to a class isn't your cup of tea, then join me in your membership area for a yoga session at www.wakethefckup.com.

CHAPTER 7

ENGINEERING YOUR BLISS

'FOLLOW YOUR BLISS AND THE UNIVERSE WILL OPEN DOORS WHERE THERE WERE ONLY WALLS.' Joseph Campbell

13 JULY 2013

'Jambo!'

This is the sound I had ringing in my ears from a small classroom filled with the cutest little children. As soon as we walked into the dusty building they started waving, screaming and singing at the tops of their voices. Their beautiful glowing smiles and big bright eyes lit up the room as they shared their adorable voices and we absorbed the sweet harmony.

'Jambo' means 'hello' in Swahili – this time my adventure had taken me to a little shantytown in Tanzania. It had taken two days' travelling to get there from London with my three suitcases filled to the brim with toys, pens, paper, letters and presents from friends back in the UK. I was with Sarah the sexy scientist and Sophie the petite brunette to film my first documentary, *One Thing Leads to Another*, a film about love, kindness and connection.

After a 12-hour minibus ride, with views of Mount Kilimanjaro and a few giraffes to spot along the way, we finally arrived at our destination. Like most adventures in life, I was making it up as I went along! Not surprisingly, two hotties and a spiritual geezer covered in tattoos, stood out like sore thumbs. Yet standing at the front of the classroom, in the middle of nowhere, I had never felt so much love and such a warm welcome from total strangers. My early conditioning and imprinted beliefs should have been telling me that Africa was a dangerous place with people who weren't at all like me, yet my heart was open and I felt more connected than ever before.

A few months before I travelled to Africa, I'd met a guy called Tony in my local gym. Tony was in his seventies and loved photography. He'd been to Africa 10 years earlier with his wife Sue to take photos on a safari trip. To cut a long story short, I overheard Tony talking about Africa in the changing rooms and how much he loved it over there. I could feel the enthusiasm, passion and energy oozing out of him and was naturally drawn to him, so I joined the conversation. Tony told me how his guide had taken him to a local school after their safari and, as he'd walked round the school and met some of the kids, something clicked inside him. He realized just how privileged his life was and how he'd lived it in a pretty selfish way, not really looking outside of his little bubble and connecting to others in need. So he decided there and then to align with his new purpose in life and told the head teacher he was going to help and support the school. When he got home he began raising money to fund the school. Asking close friends and family for small donations, he was able to pay for teachers, offer basic medical treatments and provide breakfast for the children.

'So how much do people donate, Tony,' I asked, lapping up his story and the love pouring out of him. I could literally see this peculiar energy beaming out of his eyes and it connected with my soul!

'People donate what they can, Brett, £10 or £20 here and there.'

'Wow!' I thought to myself, I'd just spent £100 just on fruit and veg so I could do a juice cleanse!

'Tony, I'd love to help. I reckon I could raise a few quid for the school and I'd love to come over there with you and help out with the kids.'

Tony smiled and told me how he was holding a sports tournament in a few months' time and the rest, as they say, is history.

I was on it like Sonic and within a few months had created an online Kickstarter campaign, pulled people together, asked for donations and raised over £4,000 to help the school and film the sports tournament. At the time I didn't know anything about cameras or making documentaries! On some of the interviews I forgot to turn on the mic, other days I forgot to charge the batteries, and we even had goats walking through our shots. But it was an adventure and I loved it!

On our travels I met hundreds of children. Played football with street kids. Connected with little toddlers and had photos taken with Masai tribespeople. But there was one little girl who has never left my heart.

I was standing in a field while about 30 children ran around me chasing a football, when out of the blue I felt a tug on the back of my T-shirt. I turned around to find a little girl holding up her arms to be picked up so I bent down and hoisted her onto my waist. As I looked into her beautiful eyes, I felt a connection to the bliss. She was around four or five, dressed in rags and with holes in her shoes, but she had a beautiful smile and so much love and happiness in her heart that I melted. Her body was dirty with dust but her cuddles were pure and priceless. I felt so much warmth and affection between us as we stood there not speaking a word, just looking into each others' eyes.

After 20 minutes or so my back started to ache and I wanted to get stuck in with the boys and play football so I leant down to put her down but she wouldn't let go of my neck. Her grip was locked tight like a wrestler and I could see how much our connection meant to her. So I picked her up again and thought nothing of it. We spent more time staring into each other's eyes and smiling. When I tried to put her down the second time, the same thing happened. She was glued to me! This time I thought she was going to cry so I picked her up again quickly. One of the teachers noticed and walked over to rescue me. She tried to prise the little girl away but her grip was too strong, so she yanked at the little girl but she wasn't having any of it and gave the teacher a dirty look. So I told the teacher not to worry about it. Then the teacher said something that changed the atmosphere within a split second: 'Her mummy and daddy are dead. She wants to stay with you now.'

For a moment I was still smiling, I thought I'd heard it wrong, then the smile on my face dropped and I said to the teacher, 'I don't understand you.'

The teacher said it again but more bluntly, 'Her mummy and daddy are dead, they died of AIDS, she lives with her grandma who is old and sick, I think she wants to stay with you forever.'

BLISS : THE DEEPER JOY THAT COMES FROM FOLLOWING YOUR PURPOSE AND LIVING WITH PASSION!

Originally this chapter was going to be called Engineering Happiness, but then I thought, f#ck that, happiness is way overrated. Everyone wants it but we often end up searching for it in all the wrong places. We get what we want – become happy – but then it's short-lived: one minute we're up and the next we're back down and wanting more. Happiness these days often seems to come with a price tag and it's losing its meaning altogether! Beyond happiness there is a deeper sense of contentment that we can feel. We can enter a blissful state! Bliss is a magnified emotional state of joy, happiness and personal fulfilment all wrapped into one. So we might as well learn how to engineer bliss and take our joy and happiness to the next level at the same time.

You know when you're connected to this blissful feeling because your ego melts away and your soul merges into the universe. You feel free, united with something special and have this cosmic feeling inside you and all around you, as the hassles of life and the never-ending rat race seem to fade into the background. As you become more practiced in emptying your mind and stepping into the bliss, you engage with life more deeply and see beyond society's illusions. Quite simply, you tune into life's wonderful buzz! As you become aware of this higher state more frequently and reconnect to it more consistently, life takes on a new perspective, doors open, you change deep inside and your days are filled with more joy and adventure.

It might seem odd to start this chapter with a story about a little girl in Africa who touched my heart so deeply. I'll admit after I came home from Africa I was pretty lost; I felt angry at and confused by the world we live in and how little kids are suffering. But once I pulled my head out of my arse, I realized what that little girl really taught me: how true bliss is all around us, it's found in our connection with one another and we ignite it when we follow our passion and make life about others. The people in Africa showed me that you can have nothing in the world, but feel happier and seem richer than some of the wealthiest people on the planet. It wasn't just the kids in Africa who had holes in their clothes and looked undernourished; the adults also walked around with less than anything I've ever seen, but they smiled from within and were happy to share everything they had with a complete stranger like me.

Yes, my heart sank when I heard about the little girl's start in life, but it also taught me to follow what I felt inspired to do and not waste any of my precious time worrying or moaning about material things. As a kid I had everything I could want: mountain bike, computer games, clean clothes, a television in my bedroom and three meals a day. The kids in the playground and the little girl I'd held in my arms were living in poverty, but they were the happiest children I had ever met.

The day we left Tanzania was the hardest part of the trip. I was moved deeply by the toddlers who picked scraps of food off rubbish tips, shocked when the street boys showed me where they lived and when their teacher told me how they'd got away from sexual abuse and drugs on the streets. I felt overwhelmed one day when I'd made a quick decision and said no to a little boy who begged me for the bottle of water in my pocket – I'd refused because there were hundreds of children standing behind him asking for the same bottle of water! But the whole experience taught me that bliss is found in our simple connections with one another, the moments we often fail to appreciate properly because we're too busy to register them or we're fiddling around trying to record them. More importantly, following your passion in life and living with a bigger purpose leads to an extraordinary feeling of joy.

You can be penniless and still feel connected the bliss!

BLISS IS AN INSIDE JOB

After coming home from Africa and re-entering a Western society, I realized that our addiction to materialism and the pressures of work and 'keeping up' are simply distracting us from the true bliss we can experience in life. But so many people are so far down the rabbit hole that living any other way fills them with fear! Hooked on little screens and chasing material needs, so many people have lost their inner spark, feel burnt out and unsure of why they they're here or what their purpose in life is. In other words, we're so busy doing our best to keep up that in the process we neglect the inner universe. We're too busy updating our status to investigate our souls!

Engineering bliss means you intentionally ignite your life from within. You pay attention to how you are feeling deep down and how the path you're on is serving you by asking yourself, is this really my passion, is this path my purpose, am I happy? I'm not going to lie to you, creating a blissful life means making some big-ass decisions. You really have to step it up if you want to feel a deep sense of joy in your life more often. You can't follow the crowd and stay on a path that doesn't excite you and expect to feel this heightened state – that's never going to tap you into the magic. Creating more bliss in your life doesn't happen by accident, nor is it something you sit back and wish for. You achieve it by crafting a life that truly fulfils you and by opening your eyes to the daily miracles that happen all around us.

THE HAPPINESS QUOTA

Over the years there have been many studies into what makes us feel more satisfied in life. The frightening thing that most experts agree on is that even though we have more stuff than ever before – designer clothes, highly paid jobs, big houses, fast cars and some pretty amazing gadgets – our levels of happiness are not rising. People are more addicted and depressed than ever before!

Popping happy pills is not going to create bliss! Zoned out and numb, people seem so caught up in this external world and keeping up with the digital times that they are losing touch with the inner spark and disconnecting from the bliss all around them. Instead of looking up at the birds and the trees, waking up and doing what excites us, or what we feel passionate about and called to do, we now live in a world where most of us have our heads down playing apps, afraid to connect with strangers or follow our dreams, judging one another, neglecting nature and our passions. If we live our lives waiting for the next external fix to make us happy and keep ignoring life's message, then life becomes flat. This makes it harder for us to feel excited about the little things in life, to get going and chase our dreams, or light the fire in our bellies.

What can be done to help us tune into the bliss on a daily basis? I believe the only way out is within. We must look inside our hearts and sense whether the path we are on is how we want to live the rest of our lives. Do we feel excited by life or flat? Chances are we didn't choose our path, so we mustn't let it define who we are and who we become. If the life path you are on is not serving your purpose and not connecting you to the joy then you must do everything within your personal power to reignite that flame and find a new way.

Society has given us so much stuff, but does it really make us any happier?

LIGHTING THE FIRE IN YOUR BELLY

Tony's passion was infectious and it inspired me into action. He was living his purpose, helping a bunch of strangers thousands of miles away. If it wasn't for the passion beaming out of him that day in the gym then chances are I would never have stopped and talked to him. Passion is the fire that makes us feel alive – you can never talk a person out of their passion and they can't wait to share it with you because it makes them feel alive. We all know people who walk around passionless, they look grey and dim, as if the life has been sucked out of them and they can't wait to share their troubles with you and we do our best to avoid them. A person with passion can light up the room and change the world.

If you choose not to connect to your passion, you might find that your life becomes a daily trudge with little joy and happiness. Each day is a struggle and feels exhausting. You end up putting so much in, working yourself into the ground for little return. Your inner spark seems to vanish; you're controlled by your negative thoughts and unaware of the addictive habits that hold you back in life.

Passion is the fire that lights your spirit. It ignites more energy, gives you more drive and direction and more purpose in life, it makes tomorrow feel even more exciting than it is. Passion is a core foundation for connecting to a truly blissful life because it leads you towards a path that makes your heart sing. If you want to feel euphoric and experience more ecstasy in your life, then follow your heart and discover what makes you tick, what makes you feel alive and gets your juices flowing. It might not be helping schools in Africa, or raising money for charitable causes, but what is it that gets you going, what could you do all day even if you didn't get paid for it?

Choosing to live with more passion means you are making choices to engage in the activities that you enjoy doing. One question to ask yourself before starting down a new path is, 'Will this bring me the most joy?' Or 'Do I feel passionate about this?' You have to decide whether it's really going to make your heart sing or whether you're just putting up with it because everybody else seems to be doing the same. Unfortunately, most people are doing tasks that suck the life out of them, in jobs that rob their energy, and relationships that take them further away from love. With more passion in your life you can transform a job into a purpose, set off fireworks in your relationships, and engage fully with each moment life has to offer. Some of the happiest and most successful people I've met are those who love what they do and do what they love. They seem to have more money, stronger relationships, deeper connections and more fun in life because they inject passion into every area of their lives. They look healthy, stay young at heart, and life works out nicely for them. Some choose to follow their passion even if it's not going to create success according to society's view of achievement. They simply do it because they couldn't live any other way, they could never deny their passion.

Are you denying yourself or designing yourself a life filled with passion? Ask the following questions:

* Am I doing something I love and enjoy?
* Do I feel passionate about what I do every day?
* Does it excite me and fill me with joy?
* Am I only doing it for the money?

....

◉ Igniting your passion

Close your eyes for a moment and think of a time in your life when you really felt passionate, excited and full of joy and energy! Maybe it was when you were a young child, when you helped out a friend, when you saved an animal, volunteered for or created a project, took the day off to write a poem or turned the volume up and made some beats. Just close your eyes, travel back in your memory and ask yourself:

* What was I doing?
* How did I feel?
* Why did do it?
* How much did I get paid?

Remember what the joy and passion felt like. Feel it in every cell of your body. Do it with a couple of memories and really get your energy flowing.

When you open your eyes, answer the questions below in your journal and be honest with yourself. Remember, this isn't about you getting annoyed, frustrated or angry with yourself because you're not living fully or you realize you're not living a passionate life. It's not about dismissing the possibility of finding passion, it's about you taking control and making new decisions for your future bliss.

* When do I feel passionate and alive?

* What activities excite me?

* What do I find deeply moving?

* What do I find deeply boring?

* What would I really like to do with my life?

* What hobbies and activities did I used to love doing?

* What hobbies and activities can I start doing?

After you've listed the activities that would bring more passion into your life, find a quiet, comfortable place where you won't be disturbed. Close your eyes and see yourself doing these things one by one. Notice how you feel, how you look, the colours and sounds, and really use your imagination to create your future. Picture it until you feel the passion bubble in your belly. Make yourself feel excited and connect to your calling! See yourself living a passionate life and silently make a decision that you will commit to creating more passion in your life.

....

I remember talking to a lovely guy in the gym a few years ago. When I asked him how his day was, his faced dropped and I could tell he wasn't in a good place. As we got chatting he told me that he had spent his whole life working hard and doing all the right things – paying his bills, getting a mortgage and paying his taxes. He got married to his wife at a young age and they both saved for their retirement so they could go off and travel the world. They planned to visit the pyramids in Egypt, go on safari in Africa and laze in the sun on the beach somewhere in Asia. The more he spoke about his dream, the more I felt like welling up – I knew something didn't match up because of his body language and his energy, which seemed low and lost. It turns out he came to the gym each day to get some headspace – he was supposed to retire that year with his beloved wife but she was dying of cancer. He had become her carer and their dream of travelling together was now impossible because his wife only had weeks to live.

Life is too short and you never know what's around the corner, so fill your days with passion now. Do what you love!

People with more passion do stuff that makes them feel good and they spend their time doing things that excite them. Whether it's ice skating, starting a business, boxing, ballet, painting, playing football, yoga, writing a blog, singing, skate-boarding, or giving back by raising money for others, they do activities that get their juices flowing. Some turn their passions into profits, while others couldn't care less but do it because it lights up their souls and connects them to something deeper than the usual rat race.

DISCOVER YOUR PURPOSE

Discovering your purpose is another key to boosting your overall life satisfaction and adding more meaning to the time you spend here. It's the difference between waking up on Monday morning with resistance and boredom, counting down the long hours till you get home, the days dragging, looking forward to the weekend so you can let your hair down or get wasted, compared to waking up with passion, excitement and joy most days, wanting extra days in the week so you can crack on with your mission, and doing what you love. Living with purpose gives you more direction and it means you live for something greater than you. There is more bliss to be found in giving than there is in receiving. In giving we open up our hearts fully and feed off other people's joy, whereas in consuming and receiving we only satisfy our ego and make it stronger. When you live for something greater than yourself and serve others, or help out in any way you can, your problems shrink and your ego loses its charge because it isn't all about you any more.

Imagine you were sent to planet Earth for a mission. I know it sounds a bit mad, but stick with me! Let's pretend that before you were born you were given a task, a mission, something only you could complete. It might be anything, to save children on the streets of London, to feed the homeless in New York, invent something that is going to shape our world, write a book, or start your own charity. Only you can pursue your purpose, no one can complete this mission for you. It's as unique as your fingerprint. Now imagine spending your whole life chasing the distractions, doing stuff because everyone else is doing it, working just to get by and never completing that one mission your life was destined for. You might get to the end of your life and realize that you never followed that calling, you never pursued your purpose and now it's too late! Imagine not achieving the one thing you were sent here to do!

I get it, maybe you don't know what that mission is yet, or you don't want to be the next Gandhi, but most people I meet feel there is a bigger purpose to their lives. They have this feeling inside them that they want to make a difference and they daydream about being the hero. We don't have to be the next Mother Teresa or Martin Luther King, all we need to do is investigate a little deeper and act on what moves us.

The ultimate purpose of life is living for something bigger than you!

The trick to finding your purpose is to follow what you feel inspired and passionate about. Then listen to your gut and do something about it. For instance, you might feel so horrified by child abuse that you become a child psychologist, so angry about pollution that you start a community project and grow your own veg, or so livid about animal cruelty that you join PETA in their fight for animal rights. Your purpose can be absolutely anything you choose it to be.

....

⊕ Discover your life purpose

Set aside some time to think about the following questions. When I do this sort of work I take a few hours out and get stuck into my journal. Write down whatever comes up to help you discover your purpose and put you in touch with your core values and the morals you live by.

* What do I care about in the world?

* What needs to change?

* What have I been through that I can draw on to help others?

* Where can I make a difference?

* What am I passionate about (animals/people/the planet ...)?
* Who really needs my help right now?
* What does my gut feeling tell me?
* How can I make a difference in the world?
* What example do I want to set for my children?

Take as long as you want to answer the questions. Just make sure you think about them and connect to your inner self rather than allowing your ego to whizz through them and give you the logical answers. Connect to your heart! Remember, this isn't a test; there are no right or wrong answers. Knowing what you believe in and stand for and doing something about it aligns you with your highest virtue. Nothing in the world can compete with someone who knows who they are and why they are here.

Once you've answered the questions above and had some time to reflect, close your eyes and relax your mind and body by focusing on your inward and outward breaths. Take three or four minutes to get comfy and let your whole body relax and sink deeper. Allow your thoughts to float away like clouds in the sky and connect to your inner self. Focus on your core, just below your belly button. Feel your inner spirit and breathe into it for a few moments. Relax. Connect. Be. When you feel relaxed and connected, ask yourself these questions:

* What is my purpose in life?
* Why was I born to do it?
* How does it make me feel?
* Who will lose out if I don't step up and do it?

Continue asking this last question over and over until you reach an answer that makes you want to jump out of your chair and makes your heart want to explode with passion. On the other hand it might make you feel angry and this might become your WHY!

••

Meet Clare

Clare is a yoga teacher and, man, are her classes hardcore! She mixes spirituality with strength and for a little lady she kicks your butt with yogi love and kindness. I met Clare through my Uncle Colin – he spoke so highly of her I had to meet her and hear her story first hand.

On Boxing Day 2004 Clare was lying on a Sri Lankan beach enjoying a massage while her little daughter played nearby. The sun was beaming down, she could hear the waves crashing on the shore and everything was tranquil. Then all of a sudden the massage lady started shaking Clare and pulled her to her feet in a panic. She told her to find her daughter and run as fast as she could.

When the Sri Lanka tsunami hit the beaches, it killed over 40,000 people and left a million more homeless. Immediately after the horrific event Clare, her daughter and other survivors began helping the locals to pick up the pieces. Clare then set up a charity called Rebuilding Sri Lanka, which has raised over £1,700,00 to rebuild villages and homes for people in need, including nine libraries for children. Clare continues to do incredible work and you can check it out by visiting www. rebuildingsrilanka.org.uk

When you choose to find your purpose, or your purpose finds you, and you follow it, you'll discover more about yourself than you would in years of coaching and therapy. In giving to others and helping, we open up our hearts and learn so much more about the human spirit. Clare has been a big inspiration for me – not just because of the amazing work she does, but also because she dreams big and never gives up!

Go where you feel drawn to. Do what moves you.

Finding your purpose takes your adventure to the next level. Instead of living in survival mode with random events happening to you, you shoot towards your highest virtue and create a lot more meaning because your life purpose steers your life towards a calling that is bigger than you and that connects you to the blissful feeling.

RECLAIMING OUR BLISS

One claim that often springs up in the happiness revolution is that children laugh over 300 times a day, while adults laugh fewer then 20 times a day! It goes without saying that when some people grow up they get way too serious, moan about pointless crap and lose the joy they once felt as children. We're too busy for that childish tomfoolery! As children we lived in bliss more often than not – we were curious, creative and connected to the world around us. Life was one epic adventure after another. We lived in the moment, smiled at the silly and simple things, made up our own little worlds, giggled when the wind blew on our face and were fascinated by everything, from the bugs in the grass to how the leaves fell from the trees. What happened to this connection? When did we stop spotting those little miracles in life?

As we grow, our patterns become stronger and the programs in our brains take over. The illusions drilled into us about life and the collective belief that 'adults need to be serious' or 'life is hard' take us away from the joy and bliss. I know I'm about to state the obvious right now, but bliss is found when you wake up and open your eyes fully so you can see with your heart. Bliss is generated when we stop, slow down and take it all in. For instance, have you ever walked through a forest and watched the herds of deer running? Or taken yourself to the beach late at night and gazed up at the stars? Or have you ever acted like a little child when you were babysitting or playing with your kids and lost yourself in the game so that nothing else in the world seemed to matter? When we step out of ourselves and into life, we connect to bliss.

Reconnect to the simple things in life and you will feel more bliss!

FINDING A CONNECTION

In Jerry Braza's book *Moment by Moment* he shares a story about his connection to his daughter and how she made him really think about the simple things in life and how they are the most precious. Reading this in prison was a life-changing insight for me because I realized that every single day of our lives we experience magical moments that we'll never get again. Until then I'd been living life with blinkers on – the bliss was always there but I was blind to it.

⊕ Spotting the simple miracles

Start to notice the simple things in your life and tell your brain to register these moments fully. For instance, you might spot a stranger smiling at you, someone opening the door for you, a friend calling you out of the blue, a colleague at work helping you with a task or an inmate sharing his burn. Each night for the next week or so, just before you go to sleep, reflect on your day and remember the things that made you happy, notice the small things you might often miss and not register. At the end of the week see how different you feel. Notice how some of the simplest of things can actually make you feel a lot happier because they make you feel more connected to life.

Make a choice right now to stop doing the things that make you unhappy and follow your joy. That's as simple as it gets! Whether it's the negative thoughts you keep thinking, the negative people in your life, the addictions, your job, the unwanted behaviours, whatever it is, let go of it. Then devote your life to doing the things that make you feel happy and bring more joy and happiness into your world. Follow your heart, because that's bliss in a nutshell! Do the things you want to do, not what you are told to do. Go to places you love and do something that ignites your soul daily.

CHAPTER 8

ENGINEERING YOUR LOVE

'YOU, YOURSELF, AS MUCH AS ANYBODY ELSE IN THE ENTIRE UNIVERSE, DESERVE YOUR LOVE AND AFFECTION.' The Buddha

15 AUGUST 2015

'Swadee Krup!'

I was back in Thailand and nothing had changed except me. As we got out of the cab the flavours of the spicy food being cooked by the street vendors and all the other smells of Bangkok hit the back of my throat. Thai girls stood in bars and foreign visitors floated around looking for a seedy night on the town. Bright neon lights advertising massages glowed above our heads and the heat made us almost instantly sweat.

'Busy ain't it, Dad?' Ella said as she walked by my side.

'Yeah it is, baby. Welcome to Bangkok!' I said as I held her hand tight and kept my eyes peeled for mopeds and tuk-tuks as we crossed the street.

We had just left Thamkrabok and the chilled spiritual vibe in the temple was the complete opposite of the hustle and bustle of the city. We spent a few days in the temple connecting with the monks and talking to the nuns about spirituality and the meaning of life. I took Ella to pray in the holy temples, we took snaps of the big Buddha statues and I felt the spiritual connection merge between us. Ella watched me take my next vow and kept our camera safe from the mischievous monkeys nearby.

I've always wanted to share the magic of Thailand with Ella, especially Thamkrabok and the spiritual connection it seems to give off, because it saved my life. Plus it's the gateway to the power of love! The Eastern way of thinking is completely different from what we find in the Western world, the external dog-eat-dog chase and the need for instant gratification, which are fed into our minds from a young age. It's like the system wants us to feel cut off from our true source while it pumps false stories into our minds, suggesting we look thinner, have more riches and consume more stuff. But in the East, it's all about waking up and connecting to the source!

I've never forced my beliefs on Ella, and I could tell she was glad we weren't staying longer then a few days in the temple, especially when she saw the hole in the floor for the toilet. But I simply wanted to plant some seeds and help her keep an open mind and see that there is more to the world than Carshalton and the cards we get dealt. I've always suggested that she ask bigger questions and challenge people, including me.

I'm not 100 per cent Buddhist; I just love some of Buddhism's kind concepts and its simple approach to life, because it can help us create more happiness and fill our hearts with more love and joy – make us more connected to the magic of life. Deep down, we all know that love can make a better world for all of us. I believe that we are all connected through the power of love and that loving who we are at a core level is hands down the ultimate goal in our transformation. Without this connection, life can become a great effort and we can lose sight of this celebration; we feel like vacant vessels struggling to make sense of it all.

Having dumped our bags in our hotel room and checked out the pool, we headed out into Bangkok's hectic nightlife to get something to eat. It was Saturday night and the place was heaving. The streets were filled with tourists buying cheap imitations, filthy children no older then five or six sitting on the ground begging for food and change, and never-ending streams of noisy traffic. I reassured Ella that everything was fine, we were safe and Daddy would always protect her and we stopped by a stall and bought some fresh watermelon.

Ella's streetwise, she takes it all in and notices things that most people wouldn't. I could see her looking around and absorbing this new world. She spotted the group of dealers who offered me cocaine and anything I wanted, a young Thai girl waiting for customers who made eye contact and smiled, and we could smell the booze from the bars, but none of it felt even slightly tempting because I had the best buzz in the world and she was holding my hand walking by my side.

We ditched Bangkok after a few nights and flew over to Ko Samui. Within five minutes of being there we agreed that we had found paradise! The sea views were breathtaking, the sun was perfect and our little hideaway was a place called Vikasa, a yoga retreat filled with happy positive people that served healthy food. I was in my element! We spent the rest of our adventure riding around the island on a moped, visiting cafes and art galleries and walking by waterfalls. At Big Buddha Beach we hired a jet ski and sped across the ocean, had a massage almost every night and while I practised yoga with like-minded souls Ella lay in Savasana pose and snored her head off.

On the plane on the way home, I asked Ella what her three top moments were. Something I always love finding out. And her answers never surprised me!

'Playing cards with you in the room, Dad, pushing each other in the pool with our clothes on and just connecting.'

LOVE: THE EPIC FEELING THAT MAKES LIFE WORTH LIVING.

It's funny, we're often so busy doing activities with our kids, taking them here and there, buying them the best that money can buy, pushing them into jobs we believe will be good for them that we fail to realize that really all they want is our time and connection, our love and affection. And it's just the same for us! We all want to feel this deep affection and priceless connection.

Sadly, way too many people get caught up in their heads, fighting with their thoughts or so busy looking at a screen, that they forget how precious the simple little moments in life really are. We spend years looking for love and connection, seeking kudos with our status updates and social media profiles, looking in all the wrong places, when it's staring us right in the face!

As I mentioned in the previous chapter, one of the stories in Jerry's Braza's book taught me about the importance of connection to our kids. It stuck with me and I woke up to the fact that the real currency in life is not fame, wealth and fortune but our connection with one another. It took me years to practise it and I'm still learning, but there's no doubt in my mind that the love in our hearts and the moments of joy that we share with one another are what matter most. As parents it's our duty to teach our children how special, loved and wonderful they are, to keep them aware and not let their minds be infected by the venom society spits at them. Let them explore and have their own wonderful adventure and do our best not to hand down our fears, limitations and the illusions wired into our brain.

When Ella was a little girl, before bedtime I would read her books by Louise Hay and Wayne Dyer about loving herself, to boost her self-esteem and show her how we are all equal and one. We've spent countless hours writing out gratitude lists, praying for love, sending our families and friends good luck and visualizing our future together. Children love this stuff; they love getting creative and using their imagination. And they already know about the importance of love; they come equipped with unconditional love in their hearts ready to share it with us and the world. Just as we did!

We craved that love and connection from our parents just as much as our children crave it from us. Some of us grow up with high self-esteem, a good self-image, feeling the love and with a positive outlook on life. Other parents simply f#ck up their kids, maybe they were f#cked up themselves, but sadly some people grow up feeling disconnected and unloved. They repeat destructive patterns in the search for love or end up in abusive relationships or addicted to drugs or isolated, institutionalized or alone.

Over the years I've witnessed the unconditional love in Ella's heart express itself naturally. Like the day she gave the last slice of her birthday cake to a homeless guy sitting in the freezing cold, the time she saw an Indian lady sobbing on a busy train and went to get her a tissue to wipe away her tears, and the evening in Bangkok when she put a few slices of her pizza in a box to give to the little children begging in the street, and it's all been off her own back because that's what unconditional love is all about. There are no judgements or discrimination, it's a pure oneness with life and every living being on this planet. It's about giving to others and connecting fully!

FULL CIRCLE

After 10 years of waking up, working on myself and trying to do the right things, I sat on the beach in Thailand with Ella and realized I had gone full circle. I spent the first 10 years of my life being conditioned, the next 10 years believing in the cards I got dealt and following the thoughts in my head and then the last 10 years after that separating from my ego so I could reconnect to the unconditional love in my heart and experience the love all around us.

We all love feeling loved up. Being bang in love and falling head over heels in love with someone special. Love is one of life's most special gifts. It ignites that warm giddy feeling within us, opens our hearts fully and helps us reconnect to our source. The power of love is what holds the fabric of life and this epic universe together. You could say love is bliss, consciousness and energy all wrapped into one. It's intangible and so delightful when you feel connected to it! I believe we are here to experience love at such deep levels. I think love is the meaning of life and can change the world!

We feel the love when we stroke a cat. See a puppy wagging its tail. Watch our children play. Take a walk in nature or fall in love with a soul mate and have our first baby. Love can fill our hearts with joy, peace and freedom in an instant. When there is love in our lives we feel content and connected. The more you wake up, the more you realize that unconditional love is the only way forward – everything else is a distraction. Tuned into this potent power, we can connect to the oneness of life and the love in our hearts erupts and destroys our ego. Love is the universal connection that fuels and ignites this adventure and makes living worthwhile.

....

WHAT IS LOVE?

According to Google, 'What is love?' is one of the most asked questions on its search engine. Why? Because millions upon millions of people crave this intimacy and want to feel loved, they long for this connection and dream about having true love in their lives moment by moment. We spend hours online searching for it, drown our sorrows at a bottom of the glass because we miss it, end up behind bars because we never understood it, lose our souls and become addicted, and can feel lost, lonely and afraid without it.

Everyone is hungry for love and affection.

MASTERING LOVE

Even though love can be a simple thing to engineer, it can be tricky to master and some people spend years trying to feel its presence. Without it we can lose the plot, feel alone and empty or end up stir crazy. Whether you want to discover the authentic love within you so you feel self-love or open your heart fully so you can love unconditionally, engineering love is key. This might be the hardest wake-up call in the whole of this book. You might discover something you've been trying to avoid for some time, feel afraid to look within because you've never been there before or be fearful of what will happen once you open up. Just take one step at a time and separate from your ego, because it will be so worth it!

For someone who has been on both sides of the fence – from hating myself and life, feeling totally cut off and standing on the edge of a balcony ready to jump and end it all, to now feeling so madly in love with life, deeply connected to this extraordinary emotion and high on it, despite being single and celibate for almost three years – my aim is to share with you simple concepts that will help you explode the love in your heart and really tune into the universal love unconditionally, so you too can feel more love than the Dalai Lama's cat! To do this you really have to get out of your head and connect to yourself. We all have the key within us to unlock this intoxicating power and engineer more love in our lives. When we do, the reality tunnel in which we live opens up and the problems we used to stress about seem to fade away.

THE POWER OF LOVE

From biologists to psychologists, poets to painters and chemists to spiritualists, since the beginning of time we've tried our best to understand this potent forcer. Biologists would say love is about reproduction and survival of the species. Psychologists explain love as our need for togetherness, connection and acceptance. In chemistry we can see the effects of love in the brain: MRI scans show the release of powerful chemicals and neurotransmitters that trigger feelings of excitement, euphoria, bonding and butterflies when a person thinks about being in love. All the brain scans, boyfriends, or one-night stands in the world will never give us this deep connection to the true source of love. Why? As the old saying goes, 'Love is an inside job.'

A HIT OF LOVE

Did you know love and passion trigger the same reward systems in the brain as drugs? It turns out falling in love with someone triggers endorphins that look a lot like the effects of cocaine. No wonder at the start of a relationship we describe the feeling of love as being head over heels or giddy; we become hooked! The brain actually produces a nice big hit and we feel this addiction to love instantly. We keep checking for texts, scrolling through the other person's Facebook profile to see where they are and who they are with, and feel elated when we get a text or a call – but then utterly rejected and unloved when it's all over. The honeymoon period ends and break-up is on the cards, and it can make us feel crazy or depressed because we crave the next hit. Some go from one relationship to the next because they can't sit with themselves and stay connected. They need a hit!

Rather than search for love externally, or wait for someone to come along and make you feel worthy, we need to love ourselves first.

Love is an inside job!

....

⊕ Getting loved up

Before learning the rules of self-love, let's see where you are at on the love barometer! On a scale of 1 to 100 how much would you say you love yourself, where 100 is being head over heels in love with yourself, enjoying your own company and feeling completely comfortable in your own skin; and 1 is hating yourself, feeling disconnected and empty and not even beng able to bear looking at your reflection in the mirror? What's the score that pops into your mind?

I'm not talking about the egotistical 'look at me' kind of love. Go beyond your external beauty and take a deeper journey. How much do you really love yourself at a core level?

Please don't judge yourself when you hear the answer; this is just a tool to help you evaluate how much love you currently feel before transforming your relationship with yourself. Go with the first answer that springs to mind.

....

I've asked that same question to countless clients, friends and strangers over the years. Behind closed doors most people struggle to love themselves and their numbers are pretty low. Most people often give a score of between 50 and 80. A few stretch to 90. It breaks my heart when people answer in the 20 to 30 range. Just for the record, not one adult has ever given a score of 100! I've helped so many of my clients engineer more love in their lives, but no one has looked me square in the eyes and said, 'Yes, Brett, I love myself 100 per cent.' Well, there was one special case: Ella.

It seems that as adults we get so caught up in the negative self-talk in our heads and the story we've created about ourselves, that we forget how amazing and special we really are. We become masters at putting a brave face on things yet, inside, at a deeper level, we're pretty lost and confused, empty – almost as if we were broken. But no one is really broken; it just feels that way sometimes.

When we feel truly connected and loved up with ourselves we enjoy our own company, we feel worthy and valued even if we're single. We don't need anyone else to validate us and tell us we are loved, we feel it a core level. No other feeling or sensation in the world comes close to when you can safely say, 'I love you' to yourself and mean it. Or look in the mirror and feel this immense sense of gratitude and affection.

HOLE IN THE SOUL

So why do we do such crazy things in the name of love? When we lose the connection to love, the search can become a lot like the need for drugs. And being addicted to any drug is nasty. The habit can turn you into a dependent, obsessive, dishonest person. You only have one thing on your mind and you'll do anything to get your next fix: lie, manipulate, cheat, beg and even kill for it. But when you chase love like this, like drugs, you're chasing an illusion and there'll always be something missing. An underlying need that's not being met, which will leave you feeling empty until you fill it with unconditional love for yourself.

And that's the thing: we crave love, but seem to search for it everywhere except within ourselves. This might mean we stay in a loveless relationship for years or put up with abuse from our nearest and dearest because we think it's all we deserve or there's nothing better – believing that we're unlovable, bad, broken, or that there is something wrong or missing within us. What a load of crap! Of course, this all goes on at a deeper level, the subconscious ego is having a field day and chances are we never hear ourselves say we want more love or feel unloved. But our behaviour, patterns and life experiences reflect our need to be loved and our search for belonging.

Few of us are taught how amazing and special we really are, how to love and connect to ourselves and our hearts and live from this amazing place, and so we struggle with low self-esteem, lack of confidence, a sense of worthlessness. These are all signs of this inner emptiness, this hole in the soul. The hole in the soul can come in many forms and I've seen it in most of the drug and alcohol clients I've worked with. Perhaps abused at a young age, neglected, rejected or abandoned, they took drugs or alcohol to numb the pain and fill that inner void. Even a lack of cuddles and praise from parents can send a kid down the wrong path.

But you don't have to be a drug addict or to have been through a childhood trauma to feel this inner emptiness. Some people become needy and desperate in relationships, sleeping around, seeking approval, always questioning and wondering if the other person truly loves them. I've worked with women who put up with abuse because they feel so lonely and have such a deep need to be loved and accepted that they'll take anything that seems like love. Even if it leaves them black and blue. I've also witnessed men who get so obsessed, jealous, needy, and angry in relationships that they lose the plot when a girl breaks up with them. They end up kicking off and people get hurt.

It's difficult to love others if you don't love who you are!

Don't panic if you're not feeling the love just yet. Up next you'll find out how to hardwire love back into your life, because the most important love we can give is self-love. A place where we feel loved up, content and connected. A wonderful feeling you can access and activate 24/7 wherever you are – in prison, a coffee shop, or at home in the bath, anywhere.

THE THREE STAGES OF SELF-LOVE

I'm going to keep it really simple! If you want to experience more love in your life then first focus on the number that came to mind when you did the last exercise, and take it from there. We have to become really selfish when it comes to self-love in order for us then to become selfless in our sharing of love with others. In the last few years of my transformation, I've found there are only stages to creating the deepest connection with yourself. It took me 10 years to get it, but you don't have to wait that long. When you start using the ideas coming up, your self-love, self-esteem and self-confidence will rise. First you need to acknowledge yourself and connect with yourself. Second you need to like and accept yourself exactly as you are. Third you need to engineer self-love by building a positive relationship with yourself. Let's break each one down in turn.

#1 ACKNOWLEDGE YOURSELF

When was the last time you looked at yourself in the mirror? I mean really looked and acknowledged your inner beauty and connected at a deeper level? I'm not talking about doing your hair, whacking on your make-up and looking good. And I'm certainly not talking about when you criticize yourself, the bits you don't like and when you tell yourself how horrible or old you look. I'm talking about looking deep into your eyes and going beyond your external beauty and linking to your inner spirit.

Loving yourself comes in stages. I've never met anybody who has gone from disliking themselves to loving themselves overnight. For some it takes a long time, especially if you've always focused on the external illusion of beauty. True beauty comes from within, it's not some digitally enhanced image on the front of a glossy magazine. It's inside you. In order to build a loving and positive relationship with ourselves, we really need to look at who we are and ignore what the ego tries to tell us. Accept and recognize your own inner beauty because no one in the world can do this for you. Yes, they can say you look pretty, I love you, you're amazing, but if we don't feel it deep in our core then it doesn't matter what anyone else says about our external appearance.

Meet Sandy

'I hate myself, Brett, I've had enough. I want to die!'

Sandy didn't look like your stereotypical drug addict. She was young, pretty, well groomed and had bright white teeth. She wore little make-up, looked really healthy and her skin glowed. Sandy seemed positive and bubbly when she walked into the drop-in centre, she lit up the room and turned heads. On the outside Sandy looked like she had it all together, but as we connected her eyes told me she was in pain and suffering deeply.

In our second session she told me how she hated life and had tried to kill herself a number of times. Her last attempt nearly succeeded.

'I planned it for weeks. I knew how I was going to end it and where to do it. When the day came I felt great, Brett, really at peace. I woke up early and walked down to the train tracks, put my headphones on and just lay on the tracks waiting for a train . . . but then some guy walking over the bridge nearby saw me. He came running down to save me and dragged me away. After that I don't remember much.'

My heart sank! I felt the emotion in my throat and chest and sat with her listening. Sometimes that's all people need, just someone who will listen to them without judgement.

The next visit Sandy booked a Reiki session with me. I prepared the room and Sandy jumped on the massage bed and unscrewed both of her legs. The guy from the bridge pulled her off the tracks just in time to save her life, but both of Sandy's legs were run over and mangled.

I know Sandy's story might be a bit extreme, but this is exactly what can happen when people lose that inner connection to themselves and aren't able to process the crazy emotions in their heads. Sandy felt so disconnected, struggled with her feelings, and the voices in her head almost killed her!

Self-love is the most important key to waking up. It doesn't just save our lives and make us feel comfortable in our own skins, it's also the essence of life. Life will never be one epic adventure if we are ruled by the ego and lost in our emotions. I'm hoping your situation isn't anything like Sandy's – and if it is please reach out to someone who can help, because things can get better.

Sandy got help and is now a proud mummy to a beautiful little boy. She's created a YouTube channel and shares her message about her journey out of depression to help and inspire young girls. She's even planning to come on one of my retreats!

....

⊕ Tuning into self-love

It doesn't matter where you are on the love barometer, just remind yourself of that score and make sure you have written it down in your journal so you can use it as an indication of your transformation in the coming weeks, months and years. What I would love you to do next is to go and stand in front of a mirror and stare into your eyes. Acknowledge how that makes you feel. What's the first thing your ego tells you?

This might feel a little awkward or you might find it easy, but stay there and tune out of your external looks and into your inner spirit by looking deep into your eyes. Remember the exercise in Chapter 2 (see page 44-5) where you stared at the dot and engineered consciousness. Use the same approach but this time gaze deeply into your eyes and breathe deeply and mindfully. Use the breathing exercise in the same chapter (see page 51-2) and clear your mind. If you have low self-worth and a negative self-image, your mind will probably try to feed you critical comments and take you away from this connection, but stay strong and reconnect! For now you, don't need to say anything, just acknowledge who you are at a deeper level.

....

#2 LIKE YOURSELF

Your self-image is the personal view you hold about yourself. It's how you picture yourself in your head and what you think about yourself when no one else is around. It doesn't matter how many people tell you you're beautiful, good, kind, great, confident, or wonderful, if you don't think that way, or feel it and see it yourself, then you'll never believe what others have to say about you. Your clothes, car and all the selfies in the world don't define you. Your self-image is an inside job and so whether you view yourself as beautiful, ugly, greedy, kind, selfish, generous, dumb or talented, this image will define how you think and feel about yourself and how you live your life. No one will ever talk you out of your self-image.

If you want more love and success in your life, then you need to create the best self-image possible. Think about it, if you are always beating yourself up and have a negative self-image, then you are never going to change or break patterns. When you have a positive self-image and a positive relationship with yourself then your self-confidence and self-worth rises and you become unstoppable!

There's a fine line between having a good self-image and your ego taking over. I have a friend who thinks he's a lot smarter than he is. Basically, he knows a lot of information. He comes across as being confident, some would say arrogant, but getting to know him I've discovered that he doesn't really have as much confidence and self-worth as he would like you to believe. Sometimes people overcompensate, or the ego tricks them, and they put on another mask and act out a role that portrays a positive self-image. I used to be such a Jack the lad, always the joker of the party, but deep down I had pretty low self-esteem. It doesn't matter what masks we wear, or how much information we know, if we don't hold ourselves in high esteem and have a deeper connection with our internal self-image then we'll always lack true confidence.

So do you like yourself? Or do you bully yourself? Are you beautiful and lovely? Or do you think you're stupid and odd? Remember, whatever you think about yourself, your Prover will prove it to be true – even if it isn't and you picked this self-image up along the way from parents, caregivers or the world built around you. This is why it's very important that you create the best self-image you can and hold yourself in high regard. You and only you can boost your confidence and self-worth. You need to envision a loving self-image and build a super-strong foundation within.

Depending on your self-image you'll build a positive or negative relationship with yourself. It would be impossible to be an upbeat happy-go-lucky, person if the image you have of yourself is ugly, dumb and stupid. Over the years I've heard so many people share with me how much they hate the way they look, or that they hate everything about themselves. This is their inner self-image, created by the ego, and so they lack self-esteem, they lack confidence, lose that special connection inside and bully themselves.

The only way to create a positive self-image is to be kind to yourself, to choose to love yourself exactly the way you are. You might have a vision to be fitter or thinner and that's great, but you also need to love yourself exactly the way you are right now. So whether it's your wobbly bits, a bent nose, the size of your boobs, or your odd body, you're beautiful, and your self-image is not in the mirror, it's inside your mind. It's an inside job.

◉ Creating a positive self-image

After you've spent some time accepting and acknowledging yourself in the mirror, you need to create a positive self-image. As you look into your eyes and go deeper, start to talk to yourself in a positive way. Use the positive mantras you learnt in Chapter 1, pages 13–14, and begin to change your self-image. Stand tall, pump your chest out and tell yourself you are confident, sexy, kind, loving, wonderful, beautiful, funny, caring, smart, intelligent, gorgeous, handsome and beautiful inside. Did I say beautiful twice! Well, you are. Remember, this is not ego talking, this is a genuine affection for who you are and a connection at a deeper level. If any of this sounds too far-fetched for you then just keep telling yourself the same message over and over again. Do this every time you brush your teeth, take a shower or see a mirror.

Years ago in my drugged-out days, I hated my own reflection. I could never stare at myself because I felt worthless, small and empty, and I could see how lost I was in my eyes. Then something changed and that voice inside told me to reconnect with the real me. And so I did! I started talking to myself, being kind, coaching myself, being strong and connecting to the real me inside rather then my ego and it transformed my self-image. Now I kiss the mirror and have full-blown conversations with myself because I authentically love the handsome dude looking back at me.

I know it might be tough to look in the mirror and say I love you or stare at yourself without judgement but you have to train your mind and rewire your self-image. Begin by accepting who you are and liking the person staring back at you. Give yourself positive messages and in time you'll be your best friend. It might take two weeks or two years, but in my personal experience the sooner you get on with it the faster the change. Do this every day for 30 days and watch your confidence and self-esteem rise and self-image shift.

Change the way you see yourself in your mind and you change what you see in the mirror.

People with a positive self-image seem to feel a lot happier, have a positive attitude, become more successful and enjoy their own company. They have this inner confidence and create more from life.

Even if you have to fake it 'til you make it, send yourself love and positive messages and change the image of who you are inside your head.

#3 LOVE YOURSELF

The amount of love we feel for ourselves is usually the amount of love we attract into our lives and the level of love we see around us. If you only love yourself 20 per cent, then you'll meet someone who loves themselves 20 per cent. You'll also see the world as a more dangerous, cruel place and life as a hard journey to push through each day. When you love yourself 100 per cent, you love life 100 per cent and attract that amount into your life. Remember, everything is matching how you feel inside. I'm not talking about the unconditional love you might feel for your child or pet; unconditional love goes without saying, it's a blissful bond that comes naturally to us because it is our natural state. I'm talking about the other areas of your life, your relationship, your work, and your day-to-day experiences.

What you say and think about yourself has a gigantic effect on your mood, how you show up in the world and what you do. Your inner self-talk affects all the relationships in your life and what you feel about yourself inside you pass on to others. The next stage after liking yourself is loving yourself. Creating a real deep relationship with yourself and knowing why you are here is key to having one epic life filled with love and positive vibes!

Whatever love you feel inside is what you see and receive outside.

I know it may be hard to believe that you can have a nice friendly voice inside your head, especially when most of the thoughts that whizz around are nasty, spiteful and mean. We only have to look on social media to see how people talk to themselves. How their hearts are blocked and the ego is in the driving seat. There's so much nastiness, negativity and anger being spat out, toxic words of venom. It's sad and crazy, because there is such a loving voice within all of us and the negativity and anger just comes from the ego and we don't need it.

You've learnt a number of ways in this book to talk to yourself in a more positive and constructive way so you can rewire your mindset and uplift your mood. Well, it works the other way, too. The self-hatred, critical thoughts and judgements that make you feel worse about yourself are negative mantras and they need to stop right now! Your self-esteem gets damaged and feels disconnected from the true love within you when you let this ego talk take over. The words we think and use have such an impact on how we feel. That's why the language of love is the only way forward. We need to talk from a place of love and speak with more love if we want to feel more love in our lives.

· ·

⊕ What would love say?

You've learnt how to catch your thoughts and interrupt those little thought patterns in Chapter 1. Now when you catch any negative thoughts ask yourself, 'What would love think/say/do right now?' Or when you catc yourself about to judge, act or do something that is negative, choose to say or think, 'What would love say to me right now?' or 'What would love do right now?'

I've never heard a nasty, unkind thought from the language of love. It just doesn't have that kind of vocabulary! It's too pure for nastiness. So when you catch that part of your ego that beats you up, pushes you around or gets on your case, interrupt it gently with love and kindness. Say or think, 'I love you, I love everything about you.' Every time the ego tries to pull you away from the magic. Just ask yourself, 'How can I love myself more, how can I be gentle to myself, what would love really say to me right now?'

You can do this technique standing at the mirror or when you're out and about. When you look in the mirror take a moment to breathe and relax. Stare deeply into your eyes and tune into the language of love and give yourself some love. Let love talk to you, ask yourself, 'What would love say to me right now?' Instead of listening to your critical ego when you talk or look at others, come from a place of love and ask, 'What would love say right now?' When you see life before your very eyes and watch nature, ask, 'How would love feel right now?'

This is how we engineer more love in our lives: by taking control and choosing our thoughts and reconnecting. Imagine feeling that unconditional love you feel for your children or your pets for yourself 24/7. Or feeling bursts of love explode in your body for no reason whatsoever.

The more we engineer love and self-love in our lives, the more our lives become lovable.

ONENESS

Spiritually speaking, love is unconditional, a divine oneness; everything and everyone in life is love, made from love, and is connected through the power of love. I do my best to live my life by this concept, because when the chemistry kicks in, or my biology takes over, true love goes out the window, my animal instincts kick in and people get hurt. When I'm spiritually loved up, life and living is unconditional bliss, relationships become deeper and my self-love feels insane! And the more often you connect to the love deep within you, the more you'll begin to connect to it in others too.

The truth about unconditional love is that you don't have to do anything to earn it – you don't need to feel loved by another, win it over, manipulate it, pay for it or get into bed with it. Sex is not love. Neediness is not love. Attachment is not love. Self-hate certainly is not love. The honeymoon period is great, but I'm sorry to say it is not love, my friend! If you find that you're caught up in these little illusions, then it might be time to reassess what true love means to you. Or how much you truly love yourself, because true love is only love when it is free, felt deep within, shared unconditionally and felt internally.

Look, I'm not saying we should all become saints and stop mating. Making love when you're in a loving relationship rocks! Especially if it's in my bed! On a serious note, no one owns love, or you, or gives you love, or takes it away from you, love is who and what we are!

True love is when we wake up and realize love is oneness!

Whether you believe it or agree with it, we are all connected to the same source. We all live under the same sun, share the same planet and came from the same place many moons ago. The reason we have so many wars, so much hate, violence, greed, separation and anger, is over millions of years the ego has become a lot stronger, more intense, more interested in what it can get and much better at looking out for itself. Even if that means killing other people, animals and the planet itself we live on. But the more we accept love and acknowledge the beauty in ourselves, the easier it is to break down the barriers we have been conditioned to accept. When we feel the true beauty in ourselves, we see the true beauty in others, too – no matter what their race, culture, colour or social background!

Meet Tommy

I was running a residential course with 15 young people from disadvantaged backgrounds with a few other volunteers. The kids were f#ckers, kept me up all night, got into fights and stole booze from the bar. But I loved 'em! They reminded me of myself and our connection was incredible. One day after abseiling down a cliff and making rafts, we all jumped in the minibus and headed home. One of the kids, a lad called Tommy, had been fine all day but lost the plot in the back of the bus and started punching and beating another kid. I pulled them apart, told the driver to stop and let Tommy and me out, so we could walk back – little did I realize we were still miles away from our digs!

Tommy had walked off ahead. His body language was tense as I approached him and asked, 'What the f#ck was that all about, mate?'

He turned around, with tears streaming down his face and said, 'Sorry, Brett.'

I knew he wasn't crying because he'd kicked off, there was something deeper going on, 'You ain't gotta say sorry to me, mate, what's up?'

'Today's the day my mum died four years ago and he was acting like a prick so I just hit and couldn't stop. I miss her, Brett.' The little f#cker hit my heart. I was devastated for him! We spent the next few hours talking about his mum. I asked him about his best memories and what his mum was like. He told me she was his best friend and he loved her and missed her so bad. He told me how she raced horses and loved her white horse the most, but she'd broken her back in a fall. Not long after that, she'd turned to drink and it had got the better of her.

Tommy had a brother and sister and his dad was about, but it didn't sound like he had anyone to really talk to. So I gave him a hug and held him while he cried. I'm not sure how I held my tears back, but I remember thinking how brave he was for letting go. A few minutes later, as we stood by a fence next to a field, a white horse come up to us and walked straight up to Tommy. 'That's a sign, mate,' I told him. 'Your mum's always with you and she's proud of you!'

Connection is key! It doesn't matter if you're a young gun working in the hustle and bustle of the city, a middle-aged woman bouncing around at home, a geezer on a building site, or a kid kicking off on a residential. We all seek connection, it's a biological mechanism.

You don't have to give money to homeless people if you believe it feeds their habit and doesn't sit with you morally. You don't have to judge someone because of where they come from and, like I said, you don't need to give up sex! But a smile, or a quick conversation, can make the whole world a better place. Accepting others for who they are inside instead of the external illusion they project will open up your world to new friends and endless possibilities. Getting to know other people at a deeper level always turns out better in the long run.

I go out of my way to connect to everyone and anyone. I love random conversations with strangers and have met lifelong friends through chance encounters. I believe we learn and get more from life when we open up and leave the ego at the door. When we allow our hearts to connect to other souls living this epic adventure. Being kind to one another is a must.

Unconditional love is what sets us free from our own pain and suffering and wakes us up from this rat race. The power of loving kindness and connection are today's real currency. Start random conversations more often, smile at strangers with passion and enthusiasm, ask the lady on the checkout how she's doing, show your gratitude and practise random acts of kindness. Just the other day I bought a lady a slice of cake and you could tell by the smile on her face that it made her day. It cost me £2 to make another person's day. How epic is that!

....

⊕ An act of love

Today, choose to connect to someone with love. You might pay for their coffee or carry their bags, sit down and ask them where it all went wrong or send them a text telling them how much you appreciate them. Remember, the true gift is in giving. Think about Christmas when you hand out presents and watch your loved ones light up with joy. How does that make you feel? Do it more often and it will feel as though every day is Christmas Day.

When we open up and let our hearts rather than our heads lead the way, we attract more than we could ever imagine. The system takes everything from us – our energy, money, blood, sweat, family time and tears! Let's not let it take away the true currency of life, let's reconnect and enjoy the ride!

ONE THING LEADS TO ANOTHER

Ten years to transform my life might seem like a long time to some people. But to me it seems like the blink of an eye. One minute I was banged up in prison smoking smack, the next I'm doing yoga and backpacking around Thailand with Ella. I hate to think where my life would be if I hadn't made the decision to change. Sometimes we can't see the road ahead, but we don't need to – all we need to do is listen to ourselves and trust in the process. When you take full responsibility and make the decision to change, you send a ripple out into your future and begin to transform your destiny!

The choices we make and actions we take are all connected. Today you are creating your tomorrow and tomorrow you are creating your future, so what will it be? Will you step it up and take a leap, will you clear out the dead wood and set yourself free, will you take charge of your life and choose a new path, or will you plod on, wishing things were different?

At the end of our lives we'll think more deeply about the road we took and the life we lived. Some people may not pay their future much attention now, but it will soon come around and I'm sure we'll all ask those big-ass life questions. Was the life I lived the best it could be? Did I show up fully and follow my heart? Did I add value to the world and make a change where I could? Did I live with passion and purpose? More importantly, did I open my heart fully and connect deeply?

I have this peculiar feeling that right before the spirit leaves the body, life's special memories will flash before our eyes – the times we shared with loved ones, the special moments we cherish and the proud feelings we engineered by taking control. For some people those last dying days will be filled with regret; when their lives play back in their mind, they will be reminded of lots of moments when they wished they'd paid more attention.

Will you follow your dreams and open your heart or will you keep it locked away until it's too late?

You don't have to wait until it's too late. You can ask these deeper questions right now, you can evaluate the path you are on today and be honest with yourself. Is it taking you closer to your dreams or further away from your soul's calling?

Today is the day to make bolder decisions and charge towards your goals. Today is the day you let your heart lead the way, not tomorrow! Engineering a life you love and creating one epic adventure simply means your last breath will be one to remember. It will be those special moments that will flash before your eyes, not the box sets on Netflix you sat through or the latest status you posted!

The truth is too many people already seem to be on their last breath, blinded by society's bullsh#t, swallowed up by the system, desperate for change but doing sweet f#ck all about it. Like you, I have so much to learn, but I'm certain that when we get to the end of this epic adventure we won't remember the jobs we slaved away at, the size of our house, the colour of our car, the shoes in the cupboard, how we posed for selfies. We'll think about the people we loved, the cuddles we gave, the kisses we felt, the connections we created!

If you want more from life, and who doesn't, then declare it today and make a firm decision that you're going to travel a path that truly fulfils you. Yes, it will be a rocky road, there will be many twists and turns along the way, hard choices to make, heartache and joy, but that's life. Everyone gets knocked down from time to time, but it's how you get back up again that counts. Everyone experiences highs and lows, successes and setbacks, but it's a billion times better playing your own game on your terms and heading towards a life that excites you, energizes you and fills your mind with wonder, than running on the treadmill until it's too late!

When you focus on what you want and create a vision, life has a funny way of bending reality: pointing out the path, opening new doors, bringing people into your life, showing you the next step. Discipline your mind to focus on what you want, focus on who you want to become and take daily and consistent action to make it happen. Before you know it, one thing will lead to another and you will have transformed your destiny.

Now you are zooming out and connecting to the now, to consciousness, you'll notice the disconnection from your ego too. This is great because it gives you the opportunity to stop acting or thinking in ways that go against you and will help you make your connections deeper. Before you leap forwards, remember what you've learnt and keep in mind the key areas of your transformation.

#1 BECOME CONSCIOUS OF YOUR THOUGHTS

You are not your negative and critical thoughts, they come and go, you are not your ego, it's old and outdated. Engineer your mind and take control of the energy between your ears!

Ask yourself: 'Am I a slave to my negative thoughts or am I in control of my mind?'

#2 BECOME CONSCIOUS OF YOUR CONNECTION

Are you living in the now, connected to the moment or are you stuck thinking about the past, worried about the future? Step outside of your ego and tune into the now, moment by moment!

Ask yourself: 'Am I awake, living a connected life or do I feel cut off from the magic, am I missing the moments?'

#3 BECOME CONSCIOUS OF YOUR VISION

Having a vision gives you something to get out of bed for. It separates the wandering souls from the purposeful change makers. Use the power of your imagination to turn your vision into a reality!

Ask yourself: 'Am I being pushed around by the demands of society or do I have a clear focus and am I heading towards my vision?'

#4 BECOME CONSCIOUS OF YOUR ACTIONS

You and only you can walk this new path and it's only you who will talk you out of it. Remember, your fear is an illusion; on the other side of your comfort zone are the real comforts of life!

Ask yourself: 'Am I holding myself back from what my heart really wants or am I facing my fears and waking the f#ck up?'

#5 BECOME CONSCIOUS OF YOUR BEHAVIOURS

We are habitual creatures wired to follow patterns. But this doesn't have to be a hindrance; it can be a blessing in disguise. Engineer new patterns into your life and throw away the cards you were dealt.

Ask yourself: 'Am I repeating patterns or creating new habits? Am I acting like a robot or do I feel in control of my life?'

#6 BECOME CONSCIOUS OF YOUR ENERGY

If you feel low, flat and drained and your inner spark has faded, then treat this as a sign. You can either stay on the same old path or ignite your energy by doing something you love.

Ask yourself: 'Do I feel alive right now or am I running on reserves? Is my inner light shining bright or has it dimmed?'

#7 BECOME CONSCIOUS OF YOUR BLISS

Living with passion and purpose is no accident. We are all engineering our lives and creating our destiny whether we are aware of it or not. Living with passion and purpose will take you higher than ever before and help you rise above the rat race!

Ask yourself: 'Am I following my bliss or am I lost in the mist?'

#8 BECOME CONSCIOUS OF YOUR LOVE

We all hunger for love, we need love and yearn for love every moment of our waking lives. But love is all around us – and within us. We don't need to do anything to earn it or find it, we simply need to look within and open our heart!

Ask yourself: 'Am I cutting myself or others off from my love?'

SEEING THROUGH THE ILLUSIONS

Life is meant to be lived in awe, abundance and wonder. We were born free and designed to feel alive, energetic, vibrant and joyful. Anything else is an illusion. Deep down we are curious creatures seeking adventure. Whether it's following your crazy visions and heading towards your wildest dreams, finding your purpose in life, connecting with your soul mate, being there for your children as they grow up, or working towards better health and a deeper connection with your inner spirit and the world around you.

When we stop, look within, and pay attention to the inner and outer universe, we discover there is something far greater at play and something far bigger than this woolly daydream that society has pulled over our eyes. Something powerful, authentic and loving is bubbling up and pulling millions of people all around the world, nudging us forwards, urging us to access our personal power and step it up. Life wants us to grow and flow with nature. This epic adventure is about igniting the process of transformation so that we can wake up and spiral upwards to higher levels of consciousness. It is our curiosity and excitement that drives us forward, pushing the boundaries of humanity and raising the bar for the next generation.

One by one we have a duty to wake up, to honour our inner calling, to appreciate this beautiful life and enjoy it in whatever way we feel drawn to. We know the magic of life is found in the precious, simple little moments. Life can be trouble-free, or filled with stress, we can be who we want to be, or stay locked up in prison, the power lies within us to see through the illusions . . .

It's an illusion . . . to work your arse off for pennies in a job you hate. Sleepwalking through the days, feeling numb, stressed out and dissatisfied. Knowing in your heart there is more to this epic adventure but doing nothing about it. Life is yours for the taking! This adventure is about creating yourself, finding your purpose and stretching your limitless potential so you can enjoy the journey, create something you love and feel alive moment by moment.

It's an illusion . . . to be addicted to stuff. Hooked on pleasure and junk that goes out of fashion every six months because we have been fooled by marketing and advertising into believing that it will make us happy. Manipulated to look outside ourselves for happiness and joy, tricked into believing fulfilment can be found in external gratification. Bliss is an inside job! It's our birth right to feel free, content, satisfied and deeply happy for no other reason than we are alive, well and travelling this adventure. True happiness is found in moments of love and connection – you already know this, but now it's time to shake up the world.

It's an illusion . . . to believe we are separate from one another and disconnected from consciousness, or that the colour of our skin, where we were born, and our religion, traditions and culture define us. We are all connected in some way, whether it's by energy, magic, consciousness, whatever. This connection cannot be defined, sold or controlled. It is the meaning of life, the engine of evolution, and your ability to access to this magic is your ticket to true freedom.

It's an illusion . . . to deny your dreams and the visions that flash into your mind because society doesn't OK it. Silently suggesting that our thoughts and imagination are nothing but wishful thinking and that we should ignore our awareness and the visions we secretly dream about. We can tap into our future by using the power of our mind. You can create your reality and transform your destiny with daily visualization. Following your dreams is where true wealth can be found.

Now you can see through the illusions, what are you going to do about it? How can you bring change into your life?

THIS BOOK IS JUST THE BEGINNING

If you've read this far, you'll have some powerful strategies that can help you engineer your mind, body and spirit to wake up from the illusions, but they only work when you use them. Everything that happens to you or shows up in your life, and what you achieve is down to the levels of consciousness you are operating from. If you want something new, fun and exciting, then it's time to open your mind, be curious again, take more risks, bigger leaps, and step out of your comfort zone as you charge forward. I deeply believe that it is our decisions in life that define who we are and who we become.

Every positive decision followed by enthusiastic action creates better outcomes in our lives. It's common sense but not common practice. Life is simply a sequence of events, dots all joined together, moments that are created by the decisions you make. Good or bad, positive or negative, proactive or procrastinating, we either create a life we love or struggle with on indecision. Too many people are not making the decisions they know they should be making. They whine, moan and complain that life isn't working out for them. Never fully appreciating that it is they who are creating everything they encounter in their lives.

Each decision sets up a ripple of change in our future and puts us on course for a new sequence of events. Someone pops into our lives or something presents itself at the right time. Every event is connected. We might not realize it now, but every interaction is connected to the bigger picture to keep us moving along and growing into who we can truly become. A stranger you meet in passing, a random invitation to a party, or a conversation you overhear might just be your ticket out of the old and into something new. When you feel the urge to connect with a random person, or feel drawn to travel to a country, or decide you have a bigger purpose to pursue, then life wraps itself around you and everything is geared towards your pursuit into new and higher levels of consciousness.

Instead of following the patterns handed down to you, make a decision now to live at a higher level of consciousness, break through the norm, raise the game and create something new, fresh and exciting. Not only just for you but also for everyone around you, the people you are yet to meet, the children as yet unborn.

GIVING UP IS NOT AN OPTION

It may take some time for you to see and feel the change. This is why a lot of people give up just before they reap the rewards. I can't tell you how many times I've wanted to quit when writing this book, when giving up the drugs, or doing the right thing. Change doesn't happen in an instant. Often it takes time to reap the good rewards, but if you have some faith, determination and commitment, I guarantee positive results are just around the corner.

People make decisions but don't commit to them. They make them half-heartedly, set a vision, make a few new choices, change a few patterns, but when the sh#t hits the fan they fall back into their old ways and tell themselves it's too hard to raise the bar. They slip back into their comfort zone and the ego takes them hostage once again. You know when it's time for change, so what will you decide? Who will you become? What do you want to stand for?

Waking up is a continuous journey and it is inevitable that we'll slip up, take a few steps back and doubt ourselves along the way. The true adventure is found in the journey, not the destination! When we feel the magic within us, when we grow, stretch, charge and fail our way forward and say, 'F#ck yeah, I gave it my all!' That's what life is all about: showing up, dusting yourself down and creating your own uniqueness.

I know that engineering your life ignites one of the best adventures you could ever dream of. The dots join up, your energy catches fire and life reveals the truth. The healthier you are, the happier you will be. Let's stand up, speak up and show one another that we can really become.

I look forward to meeting you at one of my workshops or retreats. It's time to smash it!

Brett.

ACKNOWLEDGEMENTS

Writing this book has been one of the biggest challenges I have ever taken on. I thought giving up crack was hard! I never saw myself as a writer. I hated English at school and left early without any qualifications. I couldn't wait to get out and start this epic adventure. To be honest, it bores the life out of me sitting in front of the screen. But the more I think about it, the more I realize this book wrote me. Every chapter challenged me in ways I could never have dreamed of. I had to re-experience the lessons all over again, even though I thought I was in a good space and done with the lessons many years ago.

I'd highly recommend writing a book. Even if you don't get it published or share it with the world. Gather your thoughts and start writing, because when you sit down to write a book you go on this magnificent journey of self-discovery. Writing this has been one of my most transformational experiences.

With that said, the first person I want to acknowledge is little old me, Brett Moran. I'm so grateful that I reconnected to my heart, took leaps of faith into the unknown and stuck with it. Thankfully, I faced my fears and trusted in the magic, even when I felt like giving in and people took the piss! Never ever give up, Brett-Ski. Keep dreaming brother. In fact, dream a lot bigger, my friend, because your life has only just begun!

Some say we pick our parents before we arrive on this planet. So the second person I want to acknowledge is my beautiful daughter Ella Louise. I believe Ella picked me because she saw me struggling and like most angels came down to save me from the madness. The first time I looked into her eyes and we connected I felt a level of love I had never felt before. It was so pure and connected to source. A magic I never knew existed or certainly had forgotten for a long time!

If it wasn't for you, Ella, I don't think Daddy would be where he is today. You are the kindest, funniest and most compassionate person I know. Your laughter is infectious, young lady, and your wisdom blows me away every day. I love you more than chocolate (as you know, that's a lot) and you continue to teach me about the important things in life. Simple things like fun, laughter, love and connection. Daddy is so proud of you, baby, always listen to your heart, use your imagination and remember you can be anyone you choose to be. Don't take life too seriously, you are beautiful inside and out and make sure you and Molly express yourselves!

I'm eternally grateful to my mum and dad, Sadie and Kevin. As a kid you always provided for me and did your best! And Dad, even though we aren't as close as we used to be and our egos clash, I still love you big time, mate. Thanks for grafting so hard to put food on the table and teaching me all that you knew! Mum, WOW, what can I say! You're the strongest woman I know and you've always had my back since day one. I know picking me up from police stations, seeing me black and blue and addicted to drugs must have been tough on you, but you never turned your back on me. Even now, with all my spiritual ranting and my crazy visions for life you still see me for who I am inside. I hope I've made you proud, Mum. Without you by my side, I have no idea where my life would be right now. Mum and Dad, you have both taught me so much about the importance of connection and the power of love. Thanks, guys!

One young lady I really want to thank from the top, bottom and middle of my heart is my soul sister Sasha Allenby. F#ck knows where I'd be without you, sister! You've always pierced through my crazy ego, helped me see my truth and took no crap when I questioned my path or doubted myself. I think one of the main reasons this book is finally out today is because of your belief in me and who I could become. To be honest, I wrote the book just to shut you up, matey. I love you like a sister, thanks so much for the support and encouragement over the years. I'm always there for you!

Next up are all the clients I have had the privilege to work with. From the lads in prison, to the homeless people, the addicts in drop-in centres and my private clients scattered all around the globe. Every single one of you made me who I am today. In my mind it's always been a two-way process. We're all in this together and I salute you for taking charge of your lives and stepping it up. Many of you have sent me messages thanking me for changing your life. But the truth is I was just the catalyst for your transformation, you were the ones brave enough to walk the new path and put in all the hard work! You've inspired me more than you will ever know! Keep smashing it because I still believe there is more, the best is yet to come!

Of course, I am forever grateful to the spiritual dude who ignited the spark of transformation within me: Jerry Braza! Man, without your message I'm not sure I'd be writing this book today. Your book came to me at a time when I needed it most. It opened my eyes and expanded my mind to set me on a new path. One I'm in love with! Your wisdom and simple explanations about mindfulness and meditation worked like a treat and ticked all the right boxes for me. Thanks for teaching the world about Dharma. I bow to you, brother!

Another beautiful soul I want to acknowledge is Jo Jo! This young lady has pushed me, challenged me and supported me from the day I met her. The funny thing is you came to me for coaching but you've inspired me to leap bigger time and time again. Thanks for all the spell checking, cinema laughter and craziness. See you in Bali, Jo Jo!

Thanks to Jo Lal and James and all the team at Watkins Publishing. I really appreciate your belief in my message and support for my book! I plan to smash it and do you all proud while helping as many people as we possibly can. Here's to the beginning of something truly epic!

Thanks to Sandy, my editor, for being my fairy book mother. All the phone and Skype calls and encouragement you gave helped heaps. BIG LOVE!

I also want to remember my roots and big up the old school crew too. To all my mates back in Carshalton, if you're reading this then I hope it makes sense and you get something from it, lads. I'm still the same old Brett, I've just found a new path and woken up from the bullsh#t! If I can do this, anyone can. Like any environment, Carshalton limited us and conditioned us to play the cards we were dealt. We all have the potential within us to break free and be something bigger than our conditioning. R.I.P. to the ones we lost in the madness. Hit me up on Facebook! (Unless I owe you money!)

Last, but by no means least, I want to acknowledge you, the reader. Thanks for picking up this book and investing your time, energy and money. I believe life is such a precious gift and I'm not going to waste any of your time. I'm going to lay my cards on the table, give it you straight and bare all. I guarantee that if you do just a few of the things I suggest in this book, use a couple of the tools and grasp a few of the concepts, then you'll look back in six months, or a few years, and your life will have radically transformed. I take my hat off to you because it takes a true warrior to walk the hero's path and wake up. I'm not saying it's easy, there's going to be a million and one tests along the way. But it's worth it and it's so much better than the norm. Enjoy the process of deep transformation because life really is one EPIC adventure!

TRANSFORM YOUR LIFE INTO
ONE EPIC ADVENTURE

Are you ready to take your life to the next level? As well as this book, Brett has created a free online training platform, so you can watch and download his guided meditations, powerful visualizations and yoga videos to create a calm and positive mindset.

Sign up below so you can learn how to engineer your health, ignite an abundant feeling and step into the bliss as you reconnect to the love in your heart.

Visit www.wakethefckup.com and join the tribe!

WATKINS

Sharing Wisdom Since
1893

The story of Watkins Publishing dates back to March 1893, when John M. Watkins, a scholar of esotericism, overheard his friend and teacher Madame Blavatsky lamenting the fact that there was nowhere in London to buy books on mysticism, occultism or metaphysics. At that moment Watkins was born, soon to become the home of many of the leading lights of spiritual literature, including Carl Jung, Rudolf Steiner, Alice Bailey and Chögyam Trungpa.

Today our passion for vigorous questioning is still resolute. With over 350 titles on our list, Watkins Publishing reflects the development of spiritual thinking and new science over the past 120 years. We remain at the cutting edge, committed to publishing books that change lives.

DISCOVER MORE ...

| Read our blog | Watch and listen to our authors in action | Sign up to our mailing list |

JOIN IN THE CONVERSATION

Our books celebrate conscious, passionate, wise and happy living.
Be part of the community by visiting

www.watkinspublishing.com